Out from the Shadows

INVISIBLE NO MORE

CATHEY W. LAW

This work reflects actual events in the life of the author as truthfully as recollection permits. Some events have been compressed, and some dialogue has been recreated. While all persons within are actual individuals, names and identifying characteristics have been changed to protect their privacy.

Copyright 2024 by Cathey W. Law

All rights reserved. No part of this book may be reproduced or used in any manner without written permission of the copyright owner except for the use of quotations in a book review.

For more information, address:
Catheywlaw@gmail.com
Paperback ISBN: 979-8-9908874-1-1
Ebook ISBN: 979-8-9908874-2-8
Hardcover ISBN: 979-8-9908874-0-4

Dedication:

Dedicated to DK and Ziiomi, your unwavering love has been the driving force, propelling me forward with every step. I'm profoundly grateful for your embrace during moments of uncertainty, fear, and hesitation throughout the journey of completing this memoir. Thank you, Mama Catherine, for your love and the life you've gifted me, your spirit forever dwells within my heart. To every woman who's felt confined to the shadows, know this: your time to shine is now.

"Once the storm is over, you won't remember how you made it through, how you managed to survive. You won't even be sure, whether the storm is really over. But one thing is certain. When you come out of the storm, you won't be the same person who walked in. That's what this storm's all about."
Haruki Murakami

Contents

Dedication iii

Introduction: The End Was the Beginning 1

Chapter 1: The Silent Years 9

Chapter 2: Screaming Into The Void 37

Chapter 3: The Birth of A Self-Sacrificial Woman 57

Chapter 4: When The Truth Comes Knocking 79

Chapter 5: Darkest Before the Dawn 121

Chapter 6: Climbing the Ladder to Nowhere 159

Chapter 7: More Life to Live 183

INTRODUCTION
The End Was the Beginning

How many times must you be faced with an ugly truth before you gain the courage to take action, to face it head-on, with ferocity and fire? Well, for me, it was about 50 times, more or less.

I knew my husband was cheating on me for years before I finally walked away from the marriage. *Years.* For nearly two decades, I denied the reality sitting bold and barefaced before me. And then I wasted a few more years wallowing in hope; hope that he'd stop cheating, hope that he'd treat me better, hope that he'd love me the way I desperately wanted to be loved.

For 24 years, I clawed at the doors of delusion, demanding to be let in. I had poured my entire self into my marriage. If it didn't work out, what would that say about me? My very self-worth hinged on its success. I was also deeply uncomfortable with making waves or standing up for myself. God forbid I used my voice. I didn't want to be the cause of disruption, to give my family a reason to have to step away from their own lives, even temporarily, to support me.

There were moments when I allowed the question of 'what will it take for you to leave?' to cross my mind, small pockets in time when I didn't resist reality's slow encroachment on my carefully crafted world of illusions. I'm sure the few close friends I'd confided in asked themselves the same, pondering in respectful silence when I'd finally say enough is enough. Well, one fateful day in 2010, we all got our answer.

By this point, my ex-husband and I had been married for 24 years. Even though we'd been through our share of ups and downs, mostly on account of his infidelities, I truly thought we'd turned over a new leaf. He'd promised me that his days of stepping out were over and I believed him. I knew our family was worth fighting for, and I was confident he finally knew it too.

At this time, my husband, a military man, was doing a tour in Iraq. Before he left, we had an in-depth conversation about how we'd communicate while he was away. He explained that there might be some periods during his deployment when he'd be unable to contact me. The base might be locked down, all forms of communication suspended, due to security threats, or if a soldier was killed, or committed suicide, which is a depressingly frequent occurrence (according to statistics, four times as many active duty personnel and war veterans die by suicide than in combat[1]).

His words came flashing back to me on that particular day. We usually spoke often, but it had been a few days since he'd

---

1 *https://watson.brown.edu/costsofwar/papers/2021/Suicides*

contacted us. I was understandably panicked. Had something happened to him? Was he hurt? Was he *alive*? My head buzzed with questions and worst-case scenarios, like an alarm with no snooze button. I was desperate for answers. I wracked my mind, desperately seeking relief, and then I remembered that his email was still logged in on the family computer. I decided to check if there had been any activity over the past few days, any signs of life.

I switched the accounts over to his and began anxiously searching. I found a few emails from online stores where my husband had purchased items: a video camera, a web camera and a few other things. As I scrolled through his emails, I froze, the mouse's arrow hovering over a name. It was a name I knew all too well, a name I'd spent years cursing in frustration, rage and sorrow. We'll call her Beverly. Beverly was a woman my husband had been cheating on me with for a long time, a woman he was *still* cheating on me with. A woman he was sending gifts and webcams to. He hadn't even bought a webcam for us, his family. He was ignoring us while looking for ways to stay in deeper, more intimate contact with the woman he was betraying us for.

The world fell silent around me and all I could hear was the furious beating of my heart in my ears. Here I was, nearly sick with worry for him. And for what? I imagined him sitting in a darkened room, hunched in front of a computer perusing different brands of webcams, while bombs dropped around him. I saw him watching Beverly through the computer screen, while me and my kids sat at a dinner table, mourning his absence. It felt surreal. Absurd. Even being in a war zone, where the threat of violence and death were so close you could smell it, wasn't enough to keep him loyal.

Something ripped inside me, an irreparable tear in the fabric of my life, in the tapestry of reality as I knew it. I ran to the bathroom, sat on the floor and cried hysterically. I called my sister and tried to explain to her what had happened, but could barely get the words out. The only thing I could manage to say between breathless sobs was 'I'm tired'. And God, was I tired, more exhausted than I'd ever been before in my life.

Year after year, I'd sacrificed everything I had for him, always offering up my dreams for the chopping block. All that remained of me now was a shell of the woman I'd once been, with nothing left to give. I was spent.

On the day my marriage officially fell apart, I woke up believing, with childlike conviction, that our relationship was on the mend, the wounds of the past finally growing a new, fresh layer of skin. And before the day was up, that fantasy had vanished in a puff of smoke. My husband was who he'd always been, who he'd always be: a cheater. I knew I had a choice to make. I could stay and keep pretending that one day, things would actually change. Or I could finally, *finally*, choose to take back all of the love and devotion I had let freely flow into him, and pour it right back into the source: me!

There was no doubt left in my mind of what I had to do. I'd fought and fought for years, but I knew then that the fight was over for me. There was no more forgiveness to be doled out, no more hope to be harvested. It was time to choose me, to prioritize my peace of mind over this desperate delusion I was clinging to.

When I finally walked away from my marriage, I had no idea what was waiting for me on the other side of that decision. I'd been married since I was 22. And since then, I'd done everything for this man. His life, wants, ambitions, desires and goals had been the focal point of my existence. I'd abandoned careers, friends and aspirations. I'd moved homes, cities, states, and even countries for him.

Now here I was, 46 years old, and alone without a single clue of how to navigate my new reality. For the first time in my life, I'd chosen myself. But… *now what?* Where did I go from here?

For so long, I had fooled myself into believing that if I left my husband, I was destined to be on my own for the rest of my life. My husband had shown me that I was undesirable and unworthy of love. And I swallowed that belief without question. What I had failed to realize was that I would never be alone. Even in my most difficult moments, when I felt like the loneliness might swallow me whole, I hadn't been alone.

Firstly, I had God. I experienced many dark, low moments in life when I questioned God's existence. During those times, I felt confident that even if He was out there, he'd surely turned His back on me. But He'd never abandoned me. He was always there, waiting for me to turn to Him, to trust in His plan for me. After my divorce, my faith became my compass.

I often felt lost, directionless, like I was dredging through murky waters with no clue of what was hiding just beneath the surface. But I realized quite early on that the most effective way to navigate my path forward was to lean on my faith, on God. I wouldn't always have the answers, but if I just trusted in God's purpose, I'd always have a way. I'd been misguided for so long, fighting tooth, nail and heart to please my husband instead of letting go and letting God take the reins. I learned that when I walked toward God, instead of away from Him, He ran toward me.

Secondly, I had a vast network of loving and supportive people around me, folks who bathed me in light when all I wanted to do was sink into the darkness. My sisters have always been there for me through all of life's challenges. Even when I made choices they didn't necessarily agree with (like marrying my husband, for instance), they never judged or turned away from me. Instead, they showered me with comfort and compassion, lifting me up when I needed it the most. I had friends who held me, laughed with me, cried with me, and helped guide me through low times.

Thirdly, I had myself. For so long, I was blind to my power and presence. I was a wellspring of support, devotion and strength to everyone else around me. But I hadn't learned how to access those traits for my benefit. They'd always been reserved for others. My divorce forced me to look inward and to see that I possessed the tools to love myself back to life. I didn't need to look for external validation, for outside proof that I deserved happiness, that I was worthy of living a fulfilling life. I just had to believe it.

My life, up until this point, hadn't been easy. I'd suffered immense losses. I'd been beaten and broken more times than I could count. Even though I'd managed to get up and move forward after every defeat, I'd always done it out of a sense of obligation to others. I didn't want to hurt my family, my children, or my friends. I had responsibilities and people who depended on me.

But what would happen, I wondered to myself, if this time, I healed for myself? What if I treated my life like it was something worth fighting for, like I was someone worth fighting for? What if I pursued my dreams and goals with reckless abandon, like I had my husband's? What if I let go of all of the self-limiting beliefs that I'd clung to for my whole life, and just embraced my new-found freedom?

Eventually, I stopped wondering and did just that. As it turned out, the life of my dreams had been right there, within my reach, all along.

CHAPTER 1

The Silent Years

Since the moment of my birth, my life has been a series of contradictions, a pendulum swinging back and forth between love and pain, joy and tragedy. I was born in one of those waves on December 26, 1965. On that day, as the ebb carried me into the world, the flow took my mother Catherine away; the miracle of life swaddled tenderly in the unavoidable reality of death.

I don't know if my eyes, squinting in the light of a new world, ever got a chance to see her kind face. I don't know if she held me, if a moment of love and affection passed between us before she faded away. The only thing I know for certain is that soon thereafter my father Leophas Woodard walked into our home, his face ashen and his voice low and heavy, and informed my six older sisters that our family had gained a beautiful new baby girl, but had lost a mom.

The exact circumstances of my mother's death are unclear, but it's difficult not to speculate. She was, after all, a Black woman in America. Even in our current day and age, with all of the advantages of advanced healthcare systems and technology, the Black maternal mortality rate is alarmingly high.

In 1965, things were even worse. Most hospitals in America were either integrated or in the process of becoming integrated. Unsurprisingly, not everyone was happy about this development, especially in the South where racism and segregation still reigned supreme.

In Alabama, where I was born, many institutions resisted the new requirement that they had to integrate to receive federal funding. In Mobile, the pushback was so aggressive that many hospitals simply opted to transform their rooms from shared to private. Sure, Black people could now seek care at the previously all-White institutions, but the Black and White patients would not board next to each other. One hospital even removed the seats from their lobby and created a 'medical museum', filled with Civil War-era medical supplies and instruments, to avoid having waiting rooms where Black and White people would be seated next to each other. I guess you could call it 'integration lite'.

If there was so much hostility to the idea of caring for Black patients in the same spaces as White patients, it's not hard to imagine how the quality of care may have differed too.

It troubles me to think that while giving birth to me, my mother may have suffered, that she may have tried to vocalize her pain to her doctor who shrugged those complaints off or ignored them completely. I also can't help but wonder if her death was preventable. Before she became pregnant with me, her doctor had warned her that she should try to avoid having any more children and that her body might not be able to withstand the trauma of another labor. The why is unclear: had she not received proper medical care and attention in the delivery of her other babies? She was so young, only 36 and still well within her healthy childbearing years. She'd given birth to 8 healthy babies before me: April, Anitra, Vee, Bridget, Genevieve, Celeste, Zenobia and Leophas Jr. Two of them, Zenobia and Leo, died before I was born.

My grandmother, my father's mother, was a midwife in our hometown of Coden and neighboring Bayou La Batre. She'd helped my mother during the delivery of one of my sisters. Unfortunately, she passed away shortly before I was born.

Would the outcome have been different if she'd been there? Would my mother have lived, and gone on to grow old with her daughters and grandchildren by her side? We'll never know. And truthfully, when the tragedy of her death happened, our family didn't have the time to sit around and wonder about what went wrong. They had a funeral to arrange, a newborn to tend to, a whole brood of little girls to care for and their shock and grief to process.

After my mother died, a family meeting was held. My father already had six girls at home ranging in age from 3 to 17. He couldn't take care of an infant on his own, while also raising his other daughters. It was decided then that my sisters Genevieve and Celeste, who were 3 and 4 would live with my father's sister, Marguerite. My oldest sister April, who was getting ready to head off to college, wanted to stay home and raise me, but my father wouldn't hear it. He insisted that she go to school, as planned, and get her education. My dad's other sister, Mae Louise, or Aunt Ise as we called her, who was already in her late 50s at the time, took me in instead.

My sisters and I had lost our mother too early and too young. But our community surrounded us with love. We've all heard the saying that it takes a village to raise a child, and in our little coastal town in Alabama, that's precisely what we created.

I grew up in the neighboring communities of Coden and Bayou La Batre, both sleepy fishing towns on the southern coast of Alabama, located along the salty waters of the Mississippi Sound. In the 1960s, the population of Bayou La Batre was just over 2,500, though it's since declined.[2] Known as the 'seafood capital of Alabama', our little coastal city is famous for its shrimping industry. It even made a cameo in the movie Forrest Gump, as the hometown of Forrest's best friend Bubba, and later Forrest's own home when he became a shrimp boat captain.

The shrimping industry also attracted thousands of refugees and immigrants from Asian countries, like Vietnam, Cambodia and Laos, who were fleeing conflict, war and violence in their homelands. For many families, their lives and livelihoods had always been tethered to the sea. And in Bayou La Batre, they did the only work they'd ever known how to do – fish. Their

---

2 *https://www2.census.gov/library/publications/decennial/1960/population-volume-1/vol-01-02-c.pdf*

integration into the southern town wasn't without its faults though. It was still the American South, after all. At one point, members of the Ku Klux Klan even set fire to boats belonging to Vietnamese immigrants, making no secret of their disdain for the Asian communities.

As a kid, I didn't understand much about the racial dynamics of my little town, let alone America as a whole. Being Black wasn't something I thought about, it was just what I was, a reality as intimate and unchangeable as the blood running through my veins. My father didn't spend a lot of time explaining to us what it meant to be young Black girls in America, that we would have to work twice as hard to gain the same respect and recognition as our White counterparts. He just encouraged us to work hard, to pursue an education and to make something of ourselves. But still, even if he didn't tell us that the world would treat us differently, that same world was intent on reminding us every day.

I was first exposed to that reality when I was in the first grade. I came home from school one day, my clothes covered in dirt and dust. My Aunt Ise, who I lived with at the time, looked me up and down, inspecting my filthy attire. "Why are your clothes so dirty?" she asked me. "They were spotless when you left the house this morning."

I shrugged, unable to answer her. After a few weeks of having this same conversation, I finally told her the truth. "Well, my clothes are dirty because I have to sit on the floor." Shock filled her face and she quickly got up to call my dad.

"Leo!" I heard her telling him. "They're making this baby girl sit on the floor!" The very next day, my dad drove me to the schoolhouse and spoke to the principal. I'm not sure what words were exchanged in the office that morning, but I was never told to sit on the floor again. After the whole situation was dealt with, I overheard my older sisters talking. "It's because she's Black, that's why they had her sitting on the floor. They let the White kids take all of the seats."

Before that, I'd never really considered that others, especially adults, might treat me differently because of the color of my skin. It was a strange notion to me, something I initially struggled to understand. But barely a year later, I found myself confronted with that same reality.

My school held a pageant every year called Little Miss Alba. In the contest, the girls who competed had male escorts from the same class. I entered that year, wearing a long, velvet green dress, the dress I'd worn as the flower girl at April's wedding, with ruffled white socks and patent leather shoes. My hair was styled into a few tidy ponytails, all tied together with colorful ribbons. I came in second place and my family was overjoyed. My sisters wanted to take photos of me, all dolled up, with my winner's sash. They told the boy who'd been my escort, a little White boy with sandy-colored hair, to stand next to me so they could take a photo. I remember the way he physically recoiled, as if disgusted by the notion. "I'm not standing by her to take no picture!" he scoffed. "Yes you are," my sister shot back before snapping the photo. Just like that, the boy's look of revulsion was written into history. That was the second time

I realized that people sometimes treated me differently than the White kids.

But truthfully, in Bayou La Batre, most of my time was spent in the Midway and Snow's Quarters neighborhoods, which was where a good majority of the Black people called home. I was always surrounded by people who looked like me, by my kinfolk. I never felt out of place or like I didn't belong, because in our quaint community, I did.

"There go Leo's girls," people would say, as my sisters and I skipped down Midway Road, where most of my relatives lived. The street was dotted with humble wooden houses, and I knew who lived in every single one. Two of my mother's sisters, as well as my maternal grandparents lived in homes along the street. There was a candy lady there who would sell my sisters and cousins our favorite dessert: cups of frozen Kool-Aid.

Aunt Ise's house was off the main road on Highway 188. It was a tiny wooden structure. There was a long, dirt driveway out front and a metal mailbox with a red handle. The inside of the house was very small and sparsely furnished, but it was always clean.

When you came in from the front door, you landed in the living room, which had a sofa, dining table, a reclining chair and a small black and white television. There was a large curtain directly in front of the living room that acted as the door to Aunt Ise's bedroom, if you could call it that, where a bed and dresser were cramped inside. I wasn't allowed to go into her room, but my childish curiosity still lured me in a few times and I remember that the smell of honey filled the tiny, compact quarters.

My bedroom, often referred to as the back room, was to the left of the living room, and it was the largest one in the house. I had a bed, a window facing the front porch and a large wooden chifforobe. Uncle Pete, who was Aunt Ise's husband, had a bedroom to the right of the living room. His room was furnished with one single bed, and a set of bunk beds, where the foster kids they often took in slept.

We had an old-fashioned hand washer for our clothes and a clothesline strung across the backyard where we hung them out to dry, while a goat, some chickens and a few rabbits darted around near our feet. I'd adopted one of the baby rabbits as a pet and named him Scuppernong after my favorite fruit, a variety of grapes native to the south. A porch wrapped around the front of the house, and Aunt Ise and I would often sit out there in metal rocking chairs, playing games like count the cars, watching languidly as the world passed us by.

Next door to Aunt Ise was my paternal grandmother's home. She died before I was born so I never got a chance to meet her. But Aunt Ise and I would go over there often, getting supplies from the kitchen or bringing over furniture or other things we needed. The house was beautiful and spacious, with two parlors, a big family room, a massive kitchen and several bedrooms.

In between the two houses was an out-of-commission drinking well which my aunt had covered with a flimsy piece of wood. Aunt

Ise always reminded me to stay away from the structure, but one day, my curiosity got the best of me. I climbed up and dropped some coins into the well. I stuck my head inside, listening for the sound of them clinking on the ground, but it never came. Fear washed over me as I realized how deep down the broken-down well fell. Needless to say, I never went near it again.

My dad and sisters lived just down the street, in one of the only brick houses in the neighborhood. My dad built the house himself after the first house he built burnt down. The house had four bedrooms, one full bathroom and one half bathroom. People who saw the house assumed that my father must have been wealthy, but he was just as poor as everyone else in the neighborhood. He was just trying to get by like everyone else, with many hungry mouths to feed and kids to clothe. He was a meticulously neat man though, and took great pride in the upkeep and maintenance of his house. He was a skilled gardener as well, so the property always looked beautiful.

Within the sturdy walls of that house, my sisters ruled everything. My dad would let them have parties often, inviting all of their friends from school over, listening to the latest music, talking about boys, clothes and cheerleading. I observed them with curiosity and admiration – the way they styled their hair and applied their makeup, the language they used, and their confidence. And they let me hang out with them, teaching me phrases and slang and introducing me to the latest music.

In my family, my dad was flexible and easy-going about most things. He was around 5'10, with a slim build and hazelnut brown skin. He had dark wavy hair that he often dyed to maintain its deep black hue, slicked back with a heap of hair gel.

He was meticulous about his appearance and the way he presented himself. Every morning, he'd get up early, wash up, iron his clothes and head out for the day to his job as the City Building Inspector for Bayou La Batre. When he was younger, he fought in WWII. After he came back, he'd decided to remain close to his mother and his sisters. His brothers, who were also veterans, left Alabama after the war, relocating to Texas, California and Florida.

He was a simple, hardworking man who I'd never seen miss a single day of work. But there were a few things he was adamant about: that we work hard and get an education, and we always attend Church.

Every Sunday morning, he'd cook us up a feast, knowing we'd be spending most of the day at Coleman Chapel AME Zion Church before making our rounds visiting family. Buttery biscuits with strawberry jam and grape jelly, fried pork chops and a pot of Kraft macaroni and cheese. It was a simple enough meal, but it came to define Sunday mornings. Even to this day, strawberry jam still conjures memories of those noisy, laughter-filled mornings with my sisters and dad.

Even though I spent countless hours at my dad's house, I lived with Aunt Ise until I was 12 years old. She was almost a senior at the time of my birth, and financially, didn't need another mouth to feed. But she never hesitated to bring me into her home and take on the monumental task of mothering me. My life in Aunt Ise's home was simple but happy.

She was a petite woman with graying hair that she usually had tied in a tight bun at the back of her head. At night, she'd unravel the knot, and her hair would fall in long, luxurious waves down her back. As she moved, the scent of roses, from the concoction she sprayed to keep her hair smooth, wafted around her, dousing her in an ethereal aura. Her gentle spirit only intensified those soft and graceful qualities. She was soft-spoken, never cursing and hardly ever raising her voice.

On Saturday afternoons, Aunt Ise would seat me down on the floor in front of her, and we'd spend the next five or six hours chatting while she ran a hot comb through my hair. When I was younger, I dreaded the moment she'd call me inside to start doing my hair, an already tedious task that took even longer because I struggled to sit still (which more often than not led to a burnt ear or two). But the older I got, the more I came to cherish those afternoons with Aunt Ise.

After she finished straightening my hair and tying it up into a lopsided ponytail, I wasn't allowed to go back outside where I risked running around with the other kids, the sweat lifting my hair into a frizzy mess, undoing all of Aunt Ise's hard work. Instead, I'd sit at the organ in the living room, trying to teach myself to play. Or I'd lose myself in a book. I was a voracious reader, even at a young age.

My aunt and father had put their money together and bought me a complete set of Encyclopedia Britannica. For hours, I'd lie down and devour the pages, hungrily taking in all of the pictures and reading about foreign and faraway places that I longed to one day visit. I just knew that I was destined for more than my humble hometown. Reading allowed me to transcend my current circumstances, to rise above the life I was currently living and imagine more for myself.

After spending a few hours with my head in a book, Aunt Ise would call me into the kitchen where I'd help her start the preparations for Sunday dinner. I'd stand next to her, watching as her hands gracefully and effortlessly washed and seasoned the chicken, chopped the collard greens, peeled the yams and mixed the ingredients for her famous vanilla cake with chocolate frosting.

As she cooked, we'd talk about school, or she would explain different Bible verses to me. I'd listen to her soft voice and the steady percussion of kitchen tools clanking, while eagerly waiting for the moment when I got to lick the extra icing off the spoon.

I loved Aunt Ise's cooking. It was evident in the careful and deliberate way she handled every ingredient that her food was made with love. Even so, there was at least one occasion when I went to bed hungry. One day, I'd come home from school ravenous and I asked Aunt Ise what we were having. "Fried chicken," she told me. I skipped off to play while she finished cooking, excited for the meal. A little while later, Aunt Ise, Uncle Pete and I all sat down at the dinner table to eat.

Aunt Ise set down the platter of 'chicken' and I dropped my fork in shock, the clank ringing through the house. I knew what chicken looked like, and the animal on that plate was most definitely not a chicken. I bolted from the table to the backyard to search for my pet rabbit, Scuppernong. But he was nowhere to be found. That night, I cried myself to sleep, hunger burning in my belly.

Despite the temporary feelings of betrayal I felt at Scuppernong's death, I knew without a shadow of a doubt that Aunt Ise loved me like her own daughter. Everything she did was to ensure I was happy and well cared for. That said, most of my happy memories of life in Aunt Ise's home happened within the vacuum of our solitude, in the time we spent together as a unit. But things weren't always so simple. Aunt Ise and Uncle Pete were also foster parents, so there were often other kids living in the home with us too. They didn't always take kindly to the extra privileges I seemed to get in the house. While they were all forced to share a room with Uncle Pete, I had my own room. And Aunt Ise treated me with a bit more tenderness than she did the others, sometimes giving me the last slice of cake or an extra piece of candy. It wasn't that she treated the foster kids unkindly, it was just a different form of love and care that she expressed towards me. Aunt Ise was a warm and gentle mother figure to any child that entered her home. But our familial ties bonded us in a way that excluded the foster kids. She was the only mother I'd ever known.

When I was six years old, five siblings – two teenage boys and three girls close to me in age – moved in. Right from the jump, these kids seemed especially hostile to the idea that I got to have my own room, while they were forced to bunk together.

One warm summer afternoon, we were all out on the back porch playing, with no adults in sight. I saw the siblings whispering in a small huddle, and stealing glances in my direction. I shifted nervously, pretending not to notice. Before I knew what was happening or had time to react, the kids surrounded me, standing over me threateningly. There was a look in one of the boy's eyes that I couldn't quite identify. No one had ever looked at me that way before, a mixture of mischief and desire darkening his facial expressions and triggering an anxious flutter in my chest.

I felt a rush of panic come over me, something inside of me instinctually recognizing that something very bad was about to take place. As I stood there, paralyzed with horror, the two older boys unzipped their pants, revealing their underpants. I blushed, feeling both embarrassed to see them in their drawers and terrified that Aunt Ise or Uncle Pete might come out and catch us. But then, one of the boys pulled out his penis and my embarrassment quickly transformed into terror. The other boy pushed my head closer, bringing me face to face with his brother's genitals. I could barely breathe, and my heart felt like it was beating so loud, the whole neighborhood would hear it.

I looked over at the girls, pleadingly, for help. But they looked back at me with curiosity. I could tell by the eager looks on their faces that they wanted to see what was going to happen next.

Suddenly, the boy grabbed me by the head and thrust me forward. I immediately felt the urge to scream, cry and vomit but I couldn't move. I could barely breathe. He pressed his hips backwards and forwards, over and over again, while the other brother stood over me shouting instructions.

One of the sisters pushed forward, demanding that she get to go next. I wanted to scream at her that she was stupid, that what they were doing to me wasn't fun. The brother stopped telling me what to do to answer her.

"No. Mama said we can't do it to y'all," he said, annoyed that she'd distracted them from their sick mission.

I didn't understand what was happening or why, but I knew with certainty that it was wrong. I felt my spirit lift out of my body, and it was like I was watching the scene from above, perched a safe distance away from the horror that was taking place.

After a few minutes, they switched positions, the other brother taking a turn at this horrifying game. When they were done, one of the brothers pushed me to the ground, while the other one held his hand over my mouth to stop me from screaming. Then they pushed up my dress and pulled down my panties – the ones Aunt Ise had laid out for me that morning.

I squeezed my eyes shut, not wanting to know what they were doing, but just praying that it would be over quickly. I guess someone out there heard me because, after a few minutes, it was over.

They pulled their underwear and pants back up, and one of the boys nudged me with the toe of his shoe, telling me to get up. As I lay on the ground, my whole body limp, I forced myself to stand and hurriedly tugged my underwear back up.

The boys threatened that if I told anyone what they'd done, they'd beat me. If I thought I might find allies in their sisters, I was wrong. They were equally menacing, letting me know that if I got their brothers in trouble, they'd come for me too.

After that first time, the kids continued to abuse me, forcing me to perform oral sex on them countless times, as their sisters watched. I endured the pain for months, suffering in silence, wondering what I had done to deserve what was happening to me. I wanted to tell Aunt Ise, to tell my dad, tell anyone who might help me, but I was terrified. I wasn't only afraid that the siblings might hurt me more than they already had, I feared that my family might not believe what I told them. What if they thought I was lying, making the story up for attention? And how would they look at me if they found out what had been going on? I was only six, but I was keenly aware that their perception of me might change, that they might be upset with me or feel shame at what I'd done.

After a few months, I lost the will to endure their abuse any longer. I knew the risks, I knew that the siblings would likely come after me if I spoke up. But somehow being beaten up seemed less painful than continuing to put up with being violated in that way. I didn't want to do what the boys were forcing me to do, not ever again.

So I told Aunt Ise what had been going on. She never doubted me or questioned what I said. She was the personification of safety, love, and understanding. Despite her demeanor, as a quiet and unassuming Church-going woman, she fought hard for the people she loved. She was a warrior in her own right. And bless her soul, after she discovered what had been going on, she swung quickly into action. By the next day, the boys were out of the house and I never saw them again. The girls stayed in the house for a little while longer while the folks from the foster care system tried to find somewhere else for them to live. While they were at the house, they bullied and threatened me incessantly, blaming me for breaking up their family.

Even though Aunt Ise had assured me that what happened wasn't my fault, I struggled to believe her. I was riddled with anxiety and a deep, piercing guilt. I felt I was bringing shame and pain to my family, that I was making everyone's lives more difficult. I wondered if she looked at me differently now. Was she ashamed of what I had done? I felt humiliated. I hadn't wanted to do it, but I still felt embarrassed that I had.

After the abuse, I entered a period of selective mutism, a self-imposed silence that I felt would be the answer to my problems. I wanted to disappear into the earth, to become invisible. I told myself that I had to move through life quietly. Don't make a sound, don't cause any more trouble. It was the only way I could think of to avoid burdening my family any more than I felt I already had. And at this point, I felt as though my existence in itself was troublesome enough. I spoke when spoken to, or if necessary to convey something. But otherwise, I was quiet as a mouse.

Around this same time, something else happened that only solidified guilt as a permanent fixture in my young life. By this time, my oldest sister April, who had moved to Atlanta for school, had received her Master's degree and gotten married. She and her husband Wilson bought a home in the West End of Atlanta, and I would often spend summers out there, with my sisters Celeste and Genevieve. One summer, Celeste was asking April questions about my mother and her death. Celeste was only a toddler when our mother died, and she, like me, didn't quite understand the monumental loss we'd suffered. April explained to her that while giving birth to me, she'd experienced some complications and passed away.

"So if Mama hadn't had Cathey, she would still be here with us?" Celeste asked with an inquisitive look on her face. I held my breath, the question itself stabbing at my young and sensitive heart.

"Well," April responded, her voice gentle and soft, "Yes, that's probably true." I felt my heart fall into my stomach.

The realization crashed into me like a wave, pulling me under its weight. A deluge of self-reproaching thoughts flooded my mind. I was the reason my sisters didn't have a mother anymore, the reason my father was without his wife. If I hadn't been born, my family wouldn't have suffered. My sisters would all be living under the same roof, with both of my parents. My family would be complete – without me.

I struggled with my feelings of loss. In a way, I felt I didn't have a right to my grief, at least not in any external capacity. But there was one freedom I allowed myself – the ability to dream. I'd watch my Aunt Lois with her daughter Yolanda, cooking together, and I'd imagine that I was observing myself and my mom. I envisioned us going shopping together, searching through heaps of clothes at the thrift store, or laying in bed reading books to each other. I saw us getting ice cream. I pictured her screaming my name at cheer competitions or sporting events. I thought of all the things she would have taught me, like how to cook, to sew, to put on makeup. But none of this could ever happen outside the realm of my imagination. And it was all my fault. By being born, I had robbed my family of all of those experiences as well.

I felt a crack forming between me and the people I loved, especially my father. It wasn't that I was distant from them, or they from me. But I intentionally held back from deepening our relationships, especially with my dad.

I couldn't help but wonder if when he looked at me, he saw everything he'd lost. Did he see my mother in my face? Did he wish she had lived instead of me? He never did anything to make me feel this way, as though I was somehow to blame for my mother's death. But I blamed myself and that was enough. I wanted so badly to talk to him, to ask him questions about my mother.

I wanted to know how they'd met, how their relationship had blossomed. What kind of wife and mother had she been? Did my sisters inherit their love of music and dancing from her? I saw photos of her, but I had no sense of what she was like. How tall was she? What did she look like in the morning? Did her eyes change colors in the light of the sun? What did she smell like? What did she sound like when she laughed?

I wanted to know everything about her. But I could never ask. I had already caused my family enough trouble, enough heartache. I didn't want to reopen wounds of the past, to force them to unearth painful memories for my sake.

Instead, I shrank into myself, wanting to just be invisible, to disappear somewhere I wouldn't be able to cause the people I loved any more pain. I made a vow to myself then. I'd fade into the background of my family as much as I possibly could. I'd be unproblematic. After the sexual assault ordeal, and the revelation about my mother's death, I'd caused enough trouble.

For the next few years, I moved through the world silently, spending as much time as possible on my own to avoid dragging anyone else into the muck of my life and influence.

In Bayou La Batre, I had the freedom to roam as I pleased, even as a kid. I'd hop on my bike and peddle all the way to Coden Beach. When I got there, I'd stand in front of the grand expanse of water, breathing in the salty air in large, greedy gulps. The ocean gave me a feeling of possibility – there was a big, wild world out there, waiting for me to discover. I'd ride back home feeling renewed, lifted, and for a fleeting moment, I was a blessing and not a curse.

It also motivated me to study even harder and keep my grades up. I knew that school was my ticket to getting out of Alabama. Whenever I learned about a new college or summer camp, I'd spend hours researching what it would take to attend, deciphering what I'd have to do to get there. As early as middle school, I began requesting college pamphlets. I'd read through all of them, trying to decide where I wanted to go. I had no idea what I wanted to do, but I knew I wanted to go to college.

My family seemed to agree, discovering quite early on that I wasn't built for a life of labor. I was born into a family of educators, with many of my aunts working as teachers, so going to school was always encouraged.

In Bayou La Batre, many locals would supplement their income by putting in hours at one of the local shrimp factories. For eight hours, they'd stand in front of a conveyor belt, thumping the heads off shrimp. One summer, my family decided I should go over to the factory with my aunt and cousins and make some money. The experience was a huge failure. I couldn't get the technique right and I wasted hours trying to figure it out. I didn't make any money, and it was the first and last time I worked at the factory.

I left that day feeling more motivated than ever to do well in school. I couldn't fathom spending my life standing all day in a stinky factory, my hands and clothes covered in the slimy innards of shrimp. I had to make something of myself, to make my mark on the world.

The years passed this way, with me spending most of my time alone, daydreaming about the future, my head buried in books. By this time, many of my sisters had gone off to college or started working and moved out of my dad's house. I was still living with Aunt Ise, though her health had been declining for some time.

One night, when I was 12, I went to bed, leaving Aunt Ise napping in her rocker in the living room, right outside my bedroom. She hadn't been feeling well for a few days, so Aunt Marguerite had come to stay and help take care of her. A few hours later I was awoken by the sound of Aunt Marguerite's voice repeating "Louise, Louise," in the darkness. A few seconds later, she crept up to my room and closed the door, thinking I was asleep. As I lay there, my heart thumping in my chest, I heard her pick up the telephone on the stand right outside my room.

"Leo," she whispered into the receiver, "I think Louise is gone." My dad instructed her to call the ambulance, and a few minutes later he showed up at the house too. Within minutes, the ambulance arrived and pronounced my beloved Aunt Ise dead. All the while, my family thought I was asleep, but I was listening from my bed, paralyzed in shock. At that moment, I hated how small the house was, how every sound drifted through the rooms as if the walls and doors weren't even there. I later learned that she'd suffered a massive stroke and had died in her sleep.

Aunt Ise's death hit me like a storm, upending my life in the most extreme way. I was only 12, but I was mourning the loss of another mother in my life. Since I was born, Aunt Ise had raised me and brought me up in the world. She protected me in my most vulnerable moments and did her best to give me a good life. I was devastated, unable to understand the intense grief coursing, throbbing and slicing throughout my body.

My mind was congested with anxious thoughts, and a subtle shadow of guilt. Somehow, I felt I was responsible for her death too. There was something about me that made people, mothers in particular, die. Other kids got to have moms for their whole lives. But I'd already lost two. Was there something I could have done to save her? Had I not protected and taken care of her the way she had protected and taken care of me? *Why did this keep happening to me?*

I had no idea how to process the compounding grief and trauma that had been slowly stacking up inside me. So I did what I always did, the only thing I knew how to do – I went inwards. I shrank into myself again, not wanting to get close to anyone, fearing whatever had taken my mother and Aunt Ise away from me might get them too.

After Aunt Ise's death, I moved into my dad's house down the street. There were only four of us left there now: my dad, my sisters Genevieve and Celeste, and me. But I still spent a lot of time back at Aunt Ise's home. My family expected me to care for Uncle Pete, who now found himself living alone in the small house. Every day after school, I had to go to the house and prepare dinner for him.

I'd always had a decent relationship with Uncle Pete. We weren't very close, and he didn't have a lot to teach me, but we were cordial. For most of my life, I'd wondered how Aunt Ise and Uncle Pete came to be together. She'd been married one time before, and her first husband sounded far more aligned with who I knew her to be, though I never met him. He was revered and educated and the couple had one son together, who went on to become a well-established AME Zion Minister.

Pete and Ise, on the other hand, were complete opposites. She was a respectful school teacher and a Church-going woman who never raised her voice. Uncle Pete was an unemployed alcoholic who sometimes stumbled home drunk after midnight. They were mismatched in every way.

Despite the fact I'd lived with Uncle Pete for my entire childhood, I felt troubled by this new responsibility. I wanted to take part in regular after-school activities like the other kids, and this seemed an unfair task to place upon me. But more importantly, I felt pangs of fear and anxiety crawling all over me whenever I was in that house. Everything there reminded me of Aunt Ise, and of the day she died. I missed her deeply and being there only intensified my sorrow. I tried to get in and out of the house as quickly as possible, but sometimes that was hard.

I'd usually rush over right after school to prepare a quick and easy meal. Uncle Pete and I would make small talk as I worked away in the kitchen and he sat on his chair in front of the TV. I'd quickly serve his food to him, then rush back to the kitchen to wash the dishes and wait for my dad or one of my sisters. Fortunately, this routine didn't last for too long. After a few weeks, Uncle Pete's daughters who lived out in Mississippi came to get him and took him back home with them.

Back at my dad's house, I was settling into my new way of life. Though I'd grown up with my sisters, I had never really lived with them before. And now, we were sharing the same small spaces. Sometimes we'd fight, like all sisters do, arguing about chores or clothes. But my dad was very adamant about maintaining a peaceful household, so he didn't hesitate to bring out the belt if he thought it necessary, though that wasn't a common occurrence.

On Saturday mornings, we'd blast Marvin Gaye and The Spinners and clean the entire house. We'd dust, sweep, mop, do the laundry, scrub the bathrooms and wipe down the entire kitchen. We knew that we wouldn't be allowed to turn on the TV until all of our chores were done. Soul Train played on Saturdays, and it was one of our favorite programs, and definitely the one we were least willing to miss. My sisters and I watched it religiously, practicing the dances in the living room together until we were out of breath and panting from laughter.

My sisters also taught me how to style my hair and pick out the right lipstick shade for my skin tone. I never really felt pretty growing up, but I thought my sisters were beautiful and I tried to model myself after them, to emulate their style and the way they carried themselves. And it wasn't just beauty and music that they taught me about. My sister April, who attended graduate school at the same time as Nikki Giovanni, was extremely intelligent and she was always teaching me about race issues, offering me a new lens to see the world through. I learned about the Black Power movement in the 70s by ear-mugging conversations she'd have with her friends, and every time I visited her home, I lost myself in the powerful Black images she hung on her walls, and the uplifting music that was always playing.

As my sisters taught me lessons about the world, I found myself learning more and more about myself too. Life was taking on a familiar rhythm and I was finally getting comfortable. But as with most of the happy moments I experienced in life, the feelings of contentment were short-lived. A little while after I moved back into my dad's house, I was sexually assaulted again, this time by close family members. The abuse started in my bedroom one night when a hand moved to a part of my body that it shouldn't have gone to. Gradually, the abuse escalated.

I didn't understand how this could be happening to me again. I felt completely shattered, sure that there was something wrong with me, something about me that was attracting or inviting this abuse. I didn't trust anyone, my sense of safety evaporating like water on a hot day. If the people closest to me, my own flesh and blood, could violate me in such an intense and destructive way, then what was stopping anyone else? There was nowhere for me to turn for refuge. Even my own body felt like enemy territory. It was like the world was littered with landmines, and I was always one step away from becoming collateral damage.

After nearly two years of being violated, I finally resisted. One night, when they attempted to assault me, I resisted, letting them know I wasn't going to let them keep doing this to me. And then, things moved on as if it had never happened.

I didn't tell anyone in my family about the abuse. I didn't confront the abusers about all the ways that they'd hurt me and desecrated my trust. I felt like I had to put my feelings aside and maintain a healthy relationship with them, for the rest of the family. I couldn't afford to make waves, to cause any more rifts or separations in our home.

I'd spent so many years of my life suppressing trauma, stuffing all of the pain that I'd experienced in my short life into the darkest confines of my mind. Now, I piled this latest emotional injury onto the heap inside my head and I forcefully buried it, as I always did.

I hadn't even entered high school yet, but I'd already experienced so much grief and loss. I didn't understand why bad things always seemed to happen to me, but I accepted that these were simply the cards I'd been dealt. A deep depression took hold of me, and my feelings of self-worth plummeted, my will to live fading like a morning fog.

CHAPTER 2
Screaming Into The Void

By 1980, the year I entered high school, life had thoroughly wrung out every ounce of hope I once harbored, squeezing and twisting me until I was wholly rinsed of the expectation that one day, things would be different. I'd accepted that my lot in life was to be a living punishment, karma's punching bag; peace wasn't meant to be part of my story.

For years, I'd been steadily shrinking into myself, moving languidly but deliberately away from my loved ones, from everyone who knew me and the painful truth about how I came into the world. Living in Bayou La Batre, it was easy for me to fade into the background. I knew everyone and everyone knew me, and that familiarity became the smoke that concealed me. I was hidden in plain sight.

That year, my older sister Anitra and her husband James approached my dad with a suggestion. What if I moved in with them for high school? They lived in Mobile, a city around 30 miles north of Bayou La Batre. There, I'd be exposed to so much more. I could have a fuller, more culturally rich high school experience. I could meet all of their friends, their vast community of successful, HBCU-educated Black folks who would help expand my perception of life's possibilities. High school is such a crucial time in a young person's life. It's when we begin to define ourselves, to think seriously about our place in the world, and what role we want to play.

Perhaps on some quiet level, Anitra and James sensed that I needed some mentoring, that I was in desperate need of a change of scenery. What better way to shock me out of the stupor I'd been silently drowning in than to move me to the 'big city,' away from the quiet bumble of small-town living?

It wasn't as if I'd never been away from home before. When I was younger, many of my summers were spent living with my sister April and her husband Wilson in Atlanta. I cherished those times, relishing in the long drive over with my dad and sisters Celeste and Genevieve, and the freedom April extended to us when we were there. In Atlanta, April introduced me to her friend's niece, Adrianne, and the two of us spent our days riding the bus to the library, museums and different parks, just exploring. Compared to Bayou La Batre, Atlanta might as well have been New York City.

The days of exploration came to a screeching halt in 1979 when a serial killer began murdering young Black kids in Atlanta with disturbing frequency. For a while, the authorities barely took notice, the killing of Black children hardly deemed a matter worth pursuing. But it scared the daylights out of us kids, the sudden recognition that there was someone out there *hunting* us. I remember one night while laying in bed in their home in the West End, I heard someone rummaging around in the backyard and I became paralyzed with fear, terrified that if I even breathed too loudly, the Atlanta Child Murderer might hear me, and I'd become his next victim. I didn't know then that that would be the last summer I spent in Atlanta.

But I digress. My point is, I wasn't so sheltered from the world outside of Bayou La Batre. Still, when my dad, Anitra and James approached me with the proposal, I felt torn over what to do. I loved my little close-knit family community. Despite all the pain I'd experienced here, it was still home. But I was also reaching an age where I began to crave freedom, the urge to spread my wings growing larger and more desperate every day. So in the end, perhaps a little reluctantly, I agreed to the move.

My life was tucked away into a handful of suitcases and jammed into the trunk of Anitra's car. In that short, 30-minute drive, I felt as though I'd been transported to another country. I'd been to Mobile many times before to visit my sister, my Aunt Marguerite and other extended family members. But those were short trips. Life in Mobile, despite its proximity, was so different, so foreign from Bayou La Batre.

Anitra and her family, her husband and her young son Grant, had built a beautiful and full life there, one they did their best to absorb me into. Anitra worked for the government and James was an entrepreneur. They worked very hard to provide a full and generous life for my nephew and I. Grant, for his part, was more like a little brother than a nephew to me, and was always meddling in my teenage business and getting in my way. I'd always been the youngest sibling so at first it was a little bit of an adjustment getting used to living with someone so young. But he grew on me quickly.

They had a gorgeous ranch-style home with four bedrooms – so unlike the simple wooden structures in Bayou La Batre – in the city's up-and-coming Eight Mile neighborhood.

Anitra always had a great eye for design, and her house was a perfect reflection of that talent. Every room had its own character, a personality she curated meticulously to suit the function of the space. The front room, which was meant mostly for hosting guests, was decorated with an elegant suede green sofa. In the living room, where we spent most of our time lounging and spending time as a family, there were comfy leather couches that you'd sink deep into when you sat down. The dining room was furnished with a gorgeous, cream-colored set, and a large matching china cabinet, which gave the room a tasteful and refined air.

In their house, I had my own room, which Anitra had furnished with green and pink accessories – her sorority colors. I'd never had a room so large to myself before, and I felt like I was living in a palace.

Moving to Mobile did not absolve me of any weekend chores. In fact, they intensified. Anitra was a drill sergeant when it came to cleaning and every Saturday, we were up early scrubbing down the entire house from top to bottom. I was tasked with dusting and vacuuming the whole house and cleaning the hall bathroom, and Anitra would always inspect my work at the end, making sure no speck of dirt was left uncleaned.

Despite how strict she was about cleaning, Anitra did everything to make me feel like I belonged there, like I was part of the family. She and James had both attended Alabama A&M University, which is where they'd met. There, Anitra had pledged Alpha Kappa Alpha sorority, and James, Kappa Alpha Psi Fraternity. They'd remained close with the communities they built there and introduced me to their friends, a rich community of successful Black professionals like themselves.

They got together often for BBQs, dinners, Mardi Gras balls and parades. James and his friends were avid horse riders, and one of them owned a ranch where we'd spend many warm summer evenings. There, I learned how to care for horses, how to wash and brush out their manes, and how to bathe their coats until the hair shone brilliantly. I also became a sufficient horse rider myself, slowly but surely overcoming my fear of being thrown off or trampled, with a band of Black cowboys instructing and encouraging me.

I loved seeing the camaraderie between James and his friends, the deep bonds of love and brotherhood, and the way they nurtured and poured into each other. Anitra's Sorority and Sorority sisters offered me the same opportunities for positive exposure. They were a tight clique of women who supported each other in such an empowering and inspiring way and I longed to have something like that in my life. I got to take part in AKA's Culturama Program for high school students, and they took us on outings to cultural events and college tours and even conducted etiquette classes for us.

But despite how welcoming my sister's family and their friends were to me, the sense of belonging always felt slightly out of my reach. This wasn't my community, it was Anitra's.

I felt displaced in Mobile. I was an organ transplanted into another body, and that body was failing to assimilate me. In Bayou La Batre, there was a sense of intimacy and togetherness built into the flow of everyday life. Our community was small but close, relatives and friends yoked together until we all became one big family. Whether we liked it or not, we were all bound by virtue of our proximity, both physical and familial. We knew each other's secrets. We shared each other's pain and happiness. It wasn't perfect, but it was home.

In Mobile, almost every face I saw belonged to a stranger. And at school, it was even worse. I went to Mary G. Montgomery High School in Semmes, Alabama, a 40-minute bus ride from the Eight Mile neighborhood. The drive over had me thinking that I'd be walking into a den of diversity, that I'd be around kids who looked like me. I felt giddy with anticipation. I was actually excited to begin high school, looking forward to all of the knowledge that awaited me. I loved the idea of being able to select classes myself, of looking through a list of courses and curating a schedule with all of the things I wanted to learn.

Unfortunately, my eagerness faded rather quickly, the bubble of excitement bursting as I walked the hallways of my new school. I could feel eyes all around me boring holes into my flesh, insisting with their stares that I didn't belong there. My school wasn't diverse at all. It seemed all of us non-White kids came to Semmes on the bus from communities outside of town. And when we arrived at the school, we were diluted into the largely White population.

I was one out of only a handful of Black kids, and the White kids were openly hateful. The racism I was accustomed to was usually subtle, a muted and low-key strain. At my school, it was explicit and in your face. There, the White people made no secret of their disdain for Black folks, wielding it openly like a weapon.

After a while, in some twisted, evolutionary way, I learned to adapt. I still heard them spewing the N-Word at me, their voices laced with violence and illogical rage at my mere existence. But I just did what I'd done my entire life: put my head down, focused on my school work and tried not to attract any more attention. I signed up for all advanced classes, so I had plenty to keep me distracted.

But in 1981, in my sophomore year, something happened in Mobile that added a sharp and poisonous edge to the quiet taunts in the hallway. On March 21, we woke up to the news that a young Black man had been murdered and his beaten and bloodied body was found hanging from a tree.

The lynching was committed by the United Klans of America, an Alabama-based KKK organization. A year earlier, in 1980, a white cop had been killed in a botched bank robbery in Birmingham. The suspect was a Black man named Josephus

Anderson. When the case went to trial, the jury was deadlocked, resulting in a mistrial. The case was retried and on March 20, 1981, the jury once again failed to agree on a verdict, resulting in another mistrial.

The United Klans of America had been watching the case closely, and when the jury became deadlocked for a second time, they came up with a plan to inflict their cruel retribution. If a jury wasn't going to convict Anderson, they'd find another Black man to make an example of. That night, two members of the Klan cruised around in one of Mobile's Black neighborhoods, looking for someone to punish.

At that same time, 19-year-old Michael Donald was walking out of a gas station and back towards his home, the package of cigarettes his sister had asked him to pick up in his hand. A car pulled up to him, with two young White men inside. They asked Michael for directions to a nearby club. When he stopped to help him, they pulled out a gun and forced him into the car. They proceeded to drive to the woods, where they beat him mercilessly with a tree branch and strangled him to death with a rope before slicing his throat three times. Then, they drove back to Mobile and hung his lifeless body from a tree across the street from the home of Bennie Hays, the head of the local Klan organization. They wanted everyone to know exactly who was responsible.

Following the senseless and tragic murder of Michael Donald, the tension between the Black and White communities in Mobile was high. It felt like we were teetering precariously on the edge of a large void, and the smallest whisper of conflict would send us flailing into the throes of catastrophe. Fights broke out often at school between the White and Black students, usually the boys.

I was stunned and terrified by the entire ordeal. *A lynching? In this day and age?* I wasn't so naive to believe that racism was left in the dust of American history. I knew all about the extreme violence inflicted on Black folks in the country, how White people treated the lynchings of Black people like family outings, large crowds gathering to watch, picnic baskets with packed lunches in hand. I knew that many Americans collected postcards of lynchings, souvenirs of America's shameful and vicious treatment of Black people proudly on display.

But it was still shocking to realize just how enduring and persistent it was. The lynching of Michael Donald wasn't something I was reading about in a history textbook. It was in the daily newspaper and on the evening news. It was happening in the present moment, in real-time. Would the violence against us ever end, or was I bound to be afraid forever?

I became fearful of walking alone, of being in white spaces and around White people. When the students at school sneered at me in the hallways or hissed the N-word, I felt a rush of panic. What if they decided to escalate their hatred, to make it physical? Were they happy about what had happened to Michael Donald? Were they inspired? Could I, or someone I love, be next?

These questions and worries turned over in my mind constantly, heightening my already intense anxiety. I didn't know who to turn to for help, or where to seek refuge from my thoughts and fears. I didn't have the vocabulary to articulate what I was going through, but there was an acute and pervasive sadness mixed with rage coursing through me.

It was around this time, when my feelings of disorientation and anger at the world and my life were reaching a crescendo, that I met a group of boys who would come to define my high school years. Even though we were in the same grade, they became like my big brothers.

I met Walter in my AP classes, as he was usually the only other Black person there. His family had moved to Alabama from Chicago, so his voice didn't have that familiar southern twang. Walter was bold and brave. He was stylish, in that unique and individualistic way, always decked out in colorful clothes, combinations I'd never thought to put together. We spent a lot of time studying together, being that we both came from families that were adamant about us getting a higher education.

Then there were Gary and Jarris, two stepbrothers who lived down the street from me. Gary's dad, who was married to Jarris's mom, was a DJ and they'd moved to Alabama from New York.

Gary had beautiful, dark skin and a long slender frame. He was confident and carried himself with the swagger of someone aware of just how handsome he was. He loved girls and the girls loved him back – his cool style and New York accent made him appear even more interesting and desirable.

His stepbrother Jarris was an Alabama boy, born and raised. The two could not have been more different. Where Gary was loud and boisterous, Jarris was quiet and calm. He had strong muscular arms, a sturdy, powerful frame and a sweet and boyish gap-toothed smile. He played on our school's football team, the Mary G. Montgomery Vikings.

Unlike Walter, who came from a healthy and happy two-parent household, Gary and Jarris's home life was dysfunctional and chaotic. They often opened up to me about the turbulence they experienced and the drama that ensued when their parents were under the same roof. And I listened intently, relieved that for once, it wasn't me and my family under the microscope.

I began spending all of my time outside of class with Gary, Jarris and Walter. Sometimes we'd hang out at Anitra's, but usually, we were over at Jarris and Gary's, where the boys could smoke weed. At first, I just watched them, too fearful to partake myself. As they lounged on the couch, watching TV and passing around a joint, I'd sit on the ground, my books laid out on the table in front of me, doing homework. On the weekends, we'd all go watch the Vikings play, cheering as loud as we could for Jarris. Truthfully though, we preferred going to football games at the Black high schools. It was comforting to be surrounded by our own people, by the infectiously entertaining energy and the endlessly impressive bands. Sometimes, if any of the boys were dating, their girlfriends would come around too.

When I was with them, I was carefree and joyous. They knew nothing about my past. I got to have a clean slate, to be someone new, a different girl with a different story. They didn't ask me questions about my family and I didn't feel the need to tell them. When we hung out, I let go of the burden of carrying my history. I was free.

It was so comforting to be around people who didn't look at me with that familiar and frustrating tinge of sympathy in their eyes. I wasn't the girl whose mother died giving birth to her. For the first time in my life, I was just Cathey.

One Saturday evening, we were all lying on the couch at Jarris and Gary's house when one of them suggested we walk over to the park nearby to smoke. When we got there, we sat on the ground and I ran my fingers through the cold and overgrown blades of grass. Gary put the joint to his mouth and lit the end before breathing out a large puff of smoke. I watched as the little white cylinder made its way through the circle, eventually finding its way to me.

"Come on Cathey, take a hit," Gary nudged me with his shoulder, holding out the joint. I stared at the spliff burning between his fingers, at the blackened paper, its curled edges. He held it up to my face and the smell of marijuana floated into my nostrils, loud and pungent.

I'd never had any interest in doing drugs. At this point, I'd been hanging out with the boys, watching them as they smoked, for nearly two years. And for two years, I'd never even taken a single toke. But now, as Gary held the joint in front of me, I felt pressured to take it. What if they got tired of me observing them without ever taking part in the fun? What if this was a test of our friendship, if they were sussing out whether or not I could really hang out with them?

I gulped down the hesitation sitting like a bubble at the back of my throat and took the joint. As I lifted it to my lips, Gary lit the end and told me to drag in a breath. As I did, I felt my chest tighten and my throat burn, and I coughed out a messy burst of smoke. My eyes filled with tears and I let out a flurry of noisy, wet coughs. I felt like I was choking on burnt air, like my throat was on fire. Gary, Jarris and Walter laughed hysterically as tears ran down my face and I tried to catch my breath. They pat me on the back in a congratulatory way, like I'd just accomplished something impressive.

After my lungs had adjusted to the trauma I inflicted on them, I laid back on the grass and stared up at the sky. Within a few minutes, I felt my breath slow to a whisper and all of my anxious, insecure thoughts melted into the ground beneath me. I get it, I thought to myself. I get why the guys do this so much. I felt calm, more calm than I'd ever felt before. Life felt lighter, less serious than I'd been taking it. I could laugh freely, and all of my worries suddenly seemed trivial and distant.

We lay in the grass talking and giggling for a while before going to the boys' house and jumping into Jarris' mom's car. We drove around for a while listening to music, Jarris in the driver's seat, before realizing we were ravenous with hunger.

We drove over to a nearby grocery store, all the while laughing at everything and nothing.

When we got inside, we strode the aisles confidently, without a care in the world. We got to the shelves of cereal, and something about the colorful boxes and bright lights made me feel bolder and even more confident. Someone, I can't quite remember who, picked up a box of cereal and threw it. Suddenly, we were all grabbing boxes of Rice Krispies and Froot Loops and tossing them at each other and in the air. We ran down the aisles, picking up bags of Lays Potato Chips and Ritz crackers, and seeing who could throw them the farthest. We rolled bottles of Coca-Cola and Sprite like bowling balls and ripped open bags of gummy worms and Skittles, spilling the contents right into our mouths. We made such a terrible commotion, security kicked us out of the store.

Everything about what I was doing was so out of character, so unlike me. But I kind of liked it. Wasn't that why I enjoyed hanging out with the boys as much as I did? Because they made me feel like I could be someone else, like I wasn't stuck being the girl who killed every mother she'd ever had, the girl who was sexually assaulted, the girl who was moved from home to home every few years? This was a different feeling. It was liberating. And I leaned into it, hard.

I began smoking often, picking up the habit like it was something I'd been doing my whole life. Now when I hung out with the boys, I didn't say no when they offered me the joint. I took longer pulls, and coughed less. I even learned how to roll, though my joints were usually messy and required re-rolling.

After I started smoking weed, I began skipping classes too, opting to spend time with the boys feeling light and airy rather than listening to a teacher drone on and on about things I couldn't bring myself to care about. Smoking made me feel calm and helped me quiet my mind. It silenced the anxious voice in my head that blamed me for everything that had gone wrong in my life.

On some level, deep down inside, I knew that I was going down a dangerous path. I started talking back more to Anitra, James, and the teachers. I delayed doing my chores or ignored them completely. And to hell with my homework, I didn't bother doing that either. I began to get into trouble at school too.

During my junior year, the boys and I decided to skip school one day and hang out on the bus, smoking weed for hours. At some point, we were busted and dragged into the principal's office, where we all received suspensions. At home, I was yelled at for an hour. Anitra and James were shocked that I was misbehaving in such an outrageous way. I was grounded for a few weeks, though I still snuck out to go to Jarris and Gary's house down the street.

My family grew deeply concerned, and I could hear them discussing, in hushed tones, what to do with me. I was spiraling out of control and I knew it, but I couldn't seem to stop myself. I was in a car with no brakes, speeding headfirst into a wall.

At home, the tension became thick and loaded. My sister and I nearly tiptoed around each other, hyper-aware that the smallest trigger could set either of us off. We barely spoke, and when we did, the conversation usually exploded into a yelling match and we'd both huff away in frustration.

At this same time, I was finding it harder and harder to drag myself to school. I couldn't bear to sit through my classes, and I found myself nodding off more often. Sometimes I'd walk to the bus stop, pretend to jump on, and when I thought that everyone had left the house, I'd walk right back home. I didn't get away with that for too long though, because so many of Anitra's friends were teachers at the school and they'd let her know I never got on the bus.

One day, I was feeling particularly low and decided I'd stay home from school. This time, I didn't even want to walk to the bus stop and pretend to get on. I knew that Anitra was going away on a business trip later that morning, so I climbed into my closet and waited for her to leave the house.

But my plan quickly failed when Anitra swung open the closet door to look for her clothes, which she sometimes hung there when she ran out of space in her wardrobe. There I was, sitting in between the rows of dresses and sweaters, staring up at her sheepishly.

We got into a huge argument, all of the hurt and pain we'd both been holding in erupting viciously. I knew that Anitra was trying her best, that she was doing what she could to support me. But I was so full of these confusing feelings that I couldn't explain to her because I didn't understand them myself. My sorrow and grief were like venom running through my veins, poisoning everything.

"You're not the only one who lost a mother," Anitra said to me. I suddenly recognized a pain in her eyes I hadn't seen before. She was struggling too. She knew the pain I was experiencing because she was experiencing it just as much as I was. She'd only been 15 when our mother had died. I knew how difficult it was to navigate life as a teenage girl without a mother. But because of what I was going through, I couldn't help but hear her comments through a lens of guilt and self-hatred. At that moment, it felt like all of the fears I had that my family held me responsible for the death of my mother were confirmed.

We both fell silent, empty and emotionally exhausted. Anitra left the room and I lay back on my bed, drowning in tears. I lay there in my bed long after she left for work. I sat in the empty, silent house, my mind reeling. I couldn't live here anymore, under the same roof as my sister who I now felt more sure than ever saw me as the reason our mother had died.

I needed to escape, to go somewhere I didn't feel like a burden. In the early evening, while Anitra and James were still at work and the house was empty, I packed my toothbrush and a few outfits into my backpack and left. I walked over to Jarris and Gary's house, unsure of where else to go. Jarris's mom was home at the time, and seeing my distraught face and full backpack, she sat me down and asked me what was going on.

She'd always been so caring and supportive to me, and I quickly fell apart telling her what happened. She consoled me and told me everything would be okay. She said I could stay the night at her house but she was going to call my sister and let her know that I was there. I knew she was acting out of concern but I wasn't having it. I grabbed my backpack and ran out the door, determined to not have to deal with the consequences of my actions.

For hours, I walked the streets around town. I had no idea what I was going to do or where I was going to go, but I didn't want to go home. Even though I felt a small pull of fear for my safety, it paled in comparison to the shame sitting in my chest at the thought of facing my sister.

Anitra and James eventually caught wind that I'd run away and they called the police. Soon enough, a police car pulled up beside me as I strolled languidly down the sidewalk. They asked me where I was going and I stood there silently, unsure how to answer them because I didn't know. I had no destination, nowhere to go.

The officers told me that they'd been called to pick me up. Reluctantly, I got into the car and they drove me over to the police station, where I was taken to a juvenile holding center. I'm not sure how long I sat there waiting, but it felt like hours, time passing slowly. Eventually, James came and picked me up. On the car ride home, he asked me if I thought that he and Anitra didn't love and care for me. He looked so hurt, so wounded by the mere suggestion, and my heart fluttered with affection for him. Still, I sat silently, unable to look at him or to respond. I wanted to disappear, to become invisible or to evaporate into thin air and float away from everything, my whole life.

After the whole running away incident, Anitra and I barely spoke to each other, neither of us knowing what to say. The tension and discomfort at home grew into something uninhabitable.

We had an aunt who lived in the Toulminville neighborhood in Mobile, and Anitra decided that for my senior year, it would be best if I went to live with her instead. I felt numb, knowing that it was my actions and behavior that had brought me to this point. My efforts to lay low had failed spectacularly. I'd made a big mess of everything.

At first, I was worried that I'd have to switch schools, a terrifying notion for a high school student, to go somewhere closer to where Aunt Marguerite lived, in the Toulminville area of Mobile. But the secretary at my school lived near my aunt and she agreed to drive me to and from every day.

As I moved my life from Anitra's house over to Aunt Marguerite's, I looked at what my life had become, how far I'd drifted from the one I imagined I'd be living. I didn't recognize myself anymore, I didn't recognize the girl I was becoming. I saw my future laid out before me, what it would look like if I continued on that same path. Smoking had turned me into someone I didn't know and I definitely didn't like.

My childhood traumas were like a shadow that followed me everywhere I went. I knew I couldn't outrun them, couldn't veer too far from their darkness. If I even wanted happiness, I'd have to fight for it. I'd have to fight for myself.

Something kicked in then, an inner instinct that had been lying dormant all of this time. I knew that if I didn't change directions, and reroute my path immediately, I was bound to lose everything, to lose myself. I knew I had to get my life together and my determination kicked into overdrive. I was going to make some changes, to become the Cathey I'd always wanted to be.

CHAPTER 3
The Birth of A Self-Sacrificial Woman

As I sat hunched over the kitchen table at my aunt's house, a mess of papers scattered all around me, I felt giddy with expectation. After a turbulent few years of high school, I managed to get my act together, to pull the loose threads of my academic performance into a tight and tidy knot of excellence.

I remembered the day I spent at the shrimp factory as a child, and how unequipped I was for a life like that. More importantly, it was so far from the vision I had for my life. I wanted something extraordinary. And I really believed that God's plan for me was bigger than that too. I wanted to make my family proud. I couldn't afford to make any more decisions that would stress them out. So I put my head down and got my grades back on track.

Now, the act of applying to colleges where I knew I was a shoo-in for acceptance filled me with excitement for the future. Even though I was only a junior, I was too eager to wait another year to begin applying, so I started the process early.

After moving out of Anitra's house and into Aunt Marguerite's, I managed to snap myself out of my suffocating guilt and shame, at least for a little while. And I discovered that there was still a part of me that wanted to keep living. I was able to envision a life where I actually got what I wanted, where I had goals and dreams and I accomplished them. So many of the things I'd desired for myself as a young girl returned.

I remembered the summers I'd spent living with my sister April in Atlanta. Her neighborhood was near the Atlanta University Center, the largest and oldest consortium of HBCUs in the country. Whenever we drove by the center, I saw students from Spelman, Morehouse, Clark-Atlanta and Morris Brown spill outside and I knew that one day, I'd join their ranks. I wanted to inject myself into the mass of college kids who looked like me, to be a part of that community.

Most of my sisters who attended college went to HBCUs and I saw how much it had empowered them. So for me, that was a non-negotiable. I was sick of being in classrooms where I was one of the only Black students, where I felt mostly invisible. I wanted to be around other high-achieving Black kids like me. I didn't want to continue wondering if my teachers even knew I existed or valued my presence and perspective. For years, I'd watched my White teachers give all of their extra time and attention to the White students, while I received the scraps of their awareness. For my higher education, I wanted something different.

But more than anything, I wanted the kind of atmosphere I felt sure Spelman College would offer. I pictured myself joining a community of smart and accomplished young women, sitting around discussing literature, history and psychology over coffee or cocktails. I wanted to spend my days pondering the big questions of life in a classroom of like-minded peers, to learn everything I possibly could, soaking in knowledge and information. I felt deep in my gut that that was where I belonged. That was where I'd find my home.

I applied to a few other schools too, to fall back on just in case, but Spelman was the only real option in my mind. As I sat at the kitchen table, folding applications and licking the envelopes closed, I felt the cloud of sadness that had been sitting precariously low over my life lift ever so slightly. Things were looking up. My grades had skyrocketed. I'd revived my love of learning. I'd expanded my friend circle to include kids from other local schools, and I now spent most of my time with them when I wasn't studying. And I'd just started seeing a boy named Bret, who was tall and thin with big, bright eyes. We'd only been dating a short while but I already felt the seedlings of young love sprouting inside me.

Bret attended one of the many private schools in the city, where all of the well-off Black families in that part of Alabama sent their kids. We were introduced through mutual friends and immediately hit it off. He was kind, goofy, and had a warm smile that made my heart flutter madly, as if it was made of wings.

Even though we attended different schools, we became inseparable, our friend groups melting into one another. Together with our little clique, we'd hang out after school, lounging on someone's couch watching movies or going to high school parties where I sat on his lap, giggling. We dated for the rest of that year and attended each other's senior proms.

It wasn't long before I was head over heels in love and he began to make regular appearances in my daydreams of the future. I saw myself attending college with him by my side, the two of us walking hand in hand through a dreamy tree-lined campus or stealing kisses between classes.

There were a few problems with this fantasy though. One, my dream had always been to attend Spelman, a women's college. And I'd already received early acceptance there. Unless he attended another college in the Atlanta Consortium, I wasn't sure how I could accomplish both goals — to attend my dream school and to stay with Bret. The second problem was that by our senior year, he still hadn't applied anywhere, and was torn as to where he wanted to go.

I hoped with everything inside me he'd go somewhere near Spelman so we could stay together and continue our relationship into this new phase of our lives. But eventually, he applied to Dillard, an HBCU in New Orleans.

I tried to imagine what life would be like living more than 400 miles apart from the boy I was convinced, in that young and naive way, was the love of my life. I didn't feel ready to give up on everything we'd built, or to test the waters of a long-distance relationship. I wanted to be near him. I wanted our college experiences to be tightly entwined. I wanted to study with him, celebrate as we both got the most coveted internships, and cheer each other on as we walked the stage at our graduation ceremonies. From there, we'd go on to get dream jobs, and he'd propose to me on the front lawn of the home we'd buy together. I saw my future with him laid out so clearly and I yearned for it, for the happiness that seemed etched into it like a promise.

With all of this in mind, and without telling anyone my plan, I applied to Dillard. I knew if my sisters discovered I was even considering changing my plans for a boy, they'd have a fit.

As I slipped the envelope with my application into the mailbox, a pang of uncertainty stirred in my belly. Was I really going to just do away with my lifelong goal of attending Spelman? Was I being reckless by shrugging off my dream for a boy I'd known for just a little over a year?

There was a nagging voice in my head that told me I was being crazy, that it made no sense to give up everything I'd worked so hard for. But there was another voice too, and this one had a much sharper edge. It convinced me that this might be my only shot at happiness, at the possibility of having a family of my own one day. I loved Bret and I was sure he loved me too. And wasn't this what love was all about? Compromising your happiness for the sake of something greater than yourself? I was killing my dream so that our love could grow.

And anyway, I told myself, I could still live out the life I envisioned for myself at Dillard. It was still an exceptional school, an HBCU where I'd be surrounded by smart and ambitious young Black people like me. Maybe at Dillard, I could actually have it all, the life and love that I'd craved for as long as I could remember.

A few weeks later, a large white envelope with Dillard University's trademark blue and white insignia stamped on the front arrived in my mailbox. As I opened it, I felt I was on the precipice of a life-changing decision. The letter inside would determine so many things about my future. I ripped open the top and held my breath before pulling out the contents. I skimmed the page, my eyes landing on one decisive sentence: 'I am pleased to inform you of your acceptance to Dillard University for the 1984/1985 academic year.'

I felt a confusing mixture of relief and sadness, a disquieting blend of contradictory emotions. I knew I was going to be accepted; my grades and application were perfect. But something deep inside of me had sort of hoped I wouldn't be, that by rejecting me from their institution, the decision for where I was going to school would be made for me. But now I was faced with a choice: to follow my own dream or follow my boyfriend.

In the end, I chose Bret. So as the school year came to an end, I readied myself for the move to New Orleans and to my new beginning as a student at Dillard University. I didn't give myself too much time to ponder my decision, to wonder if I'd made the right choice. I had a whole life to pack up. And I wanted to spend as much time with my family and friends as I could.

I arrived at Dillard in late August, with boxes of books and clothes stuffed into the back of my dad's car. When I stepped onto the college campus, I was immediately struck by the stifling humidity, which I'd never experienced and definitely hadn't anticipated. After swallowing down the initial burst of suffocating heat, I looked around and felt a new sensation taking over my body: excitement.

After years of drifting from home to home, of being passed from family member to family member, I was finally out on my own. I had secured stability. I wouldn't have to tell anyone where I was going, I'd have no one but myself to answer to. More importantly, now Bret and I would have so much space to explore and grow our relationship. We could spend as much time together as we wanted to, with no curfews or nosy family members to worry about. It was more freedom than I'd ever had, and I was looking forward to making the most of it.

Within our first few days at Dillard, Bret and I barely saw each other. I chalked it up to us both getting used to our new schedules and learning to navigate living in a new city. But after two weeks had passed, I sensed that our distance was something more deliberate, that Bret was intentionally withdrawing from me. I finally worked up the courage to confront him about it, and I instantly regretted it. He told me that he wanted to be single for his college years, especially as a freshman. The crux of his argument was that he didn't want our relationship to deprive us of having the full college experience.

At first, I was shocked. How could he do something so callous, so devoid of love, when I'd quite literally given up my dreams to follow him there? Before long, my shock evolved into rage, at both Bret and myself. I had, afterall, gotten myself into this mess in the first place. He'd never explicitly asked me to go to Dillard with him. I'd decided to go because I loved him. But he'd also never stopped me. He even told me it would be a good idea. He never gave me any indication that he didn't want to be with me. If he had, I'd have never changed my entire life's plan to be near him.

What made the breakup even harder was the fact that Dillard was such a small campus, so I still saw him around. I gave myself a few days to feel sorry for myself, but then I became determined to not let the breakup define this new phase of my life. I was still angry and full of regret, but I resolved to just fill my days with so many distractions that it didn't bother me. As it turned out, that wasn't too hard to do.

For one thing, I had my classes to attend, homework to do and exams to study for. Learning was what excited me most about going to university, and I wanted to make sure I was squeezing everything I could out of it. But I'd be lying if I said I didn't partake in any other college 'activities,' that I was just a focused and disciplined student. Let's just say, if there was a party, on or off campus, you could almost definitely find me there.

I also became an Alpha Phi Alpha sweetheart, which kept me busy and distracted. As a sweetheart, I was the fraternity's female face, which required a serious degree of commitment and dedication to the group. I brought the guys food and attended frat events, volunteering a big chunk of my free time to support the organization in whatever way they needed me. I didn't mind at all, as it introduced me to so many new people and kept my brain and body busy so I didn't have too much time to think about my life.

Despite a pretty rocky and unpleasant start to my freshman year, I rebounded quickly. I made a ton of new friends and successfully established myself as a fixture on campus. I also got a part time job as a hostess at a nightclub near campus to try and offset some of my financial anxieties.

Things went smoothly for a while. I worked, studied, volunteered, and socialized. I felt like I was flying high, living my best life. I was intelligent and popular. I had friends who loved and cared about me, professors who appreciated my perspective and valued my presence in their classes. I was the girl I'd always dreamt of becoming. But as I busied myself, that ominous black cloud that hung over my life had been moving dangerously close to the surface and before I knew it, a darkness descended over everything.

I couldn't simply outrun or shake off the pain of my past. The depression I'd spent most of my life grappling with returned with a blinding fury like it was on a mission to obliterate me. For the past two years, I'd done my best to drown it out to hold it underwater. But the thing was buoyant as hell, and the second I let up the pressure just a little, it bounced back with an equally determined force.

Pretty soon, my overactivity didn't work to keep me distracted from my thoughts anymore. The guilt and sorrow I felt about my mother and my childhood began returning to me in a series of terrifying flashbacks. The trauma of my life replayed in my mind as I served drinks at work. I zoned out at fraternity events, vividly recalling being raped on my aunt's porch. I couldn't shake the thought of my mother from my mind, all the shame and self-loathing I felt about her absence.

A deep and paralyzing exhaustion took over me. My limbs felt dense and heavy, and whenever I was awake, I felt like I was wading through quicksand. I began abandoning my responsibilities, unable to pull myself out of bed, to conjure the energy to move at all. I'd stay in bed for days at a time, only getting up to swallow down a sandwich my roommate Candace left for me on my bedside table.

I became a shadow of the Cathey everyone at school had come to know. Candace, and the other girls that lived in the dorms in my hallway, would take turns checking on me after class. They stood over my bed, stroking my hair, bringing me snacks and supplies, asking if there was anything they could do. I'd shake my head and thank them, before turning over in my bed.

Soon, I wasn't going to class at all and had stopped showing up to my shifts at work. Weeks would pass with me barely getting out of bed. I'd just lay there all day, alternating between weeping and sleeping.

I'd opened up to Candace about my past, about my mother and other traumatic events that had occurred in my short but layered life. And she tried her best to support me through the debilitating sadness I was suffering from. But eventually, she realized she needed to call someone for help, that her words and affection weren't enough to pull me out of the muck I was drowning in. She asked me for my dad's phone number, and though I was a little reluctant, I gave it to her.

A week or so later, my dad drove down to New Orleans to see me. I felt guilty that he'd come all that way, that I was causing such a disruption in his life. I couldn't bear for him to see the desperate state I'd been in, to cause him more worry, so I pulled myself together. We walked around campus, talking casually about what I'd been going through. I was unable to admit to him how deeply sad I was, how much I was suffering. I told him that I'd just been overwhelmed with my classes and with work and finances. I assured him that I'd be fine, I just needed to find a better balance between working and resting.

We spent the day together and then he made the two-hour drive back home to Alabama. After that, I knew I had to do something, to talk to someone. It wasn't for the sake of myself but for my family. I didn't want to burden them like this, to create situations where they needed to sacrifice their time to check on me. I needed to get better, for them.

I called my sisters Celeste and Genevieve and confessed everything. They listened, and I could sense by the kind murmur in their voices that they didn't just sympathize with what I was going through, but they understood it intimately. I got the feeling they'd been through similar journeys.

Later I spoke with April, my oldest sister, and she suggested that maybe I should transfer to Spelman, where I'd always dreamt of being. If my heart wasn't happy at Dillard, I didn't have to stay there, she assured me. People transferred schools all the time, it was no big deal. I'd just have to reapply and they would help me find an apartment in Atlanta and with all of the other logistics. She knew people who could help me find something pleasant next to Spelman.

The idea of living near my sisters again filled me with an unexpected warmth. As much as I'd loved living on my own, I missed being around family. I knew that if I wanted to transfer to Spelman, I'd need to get my grades back on track and get my act together. I was still sad and exhausted, but I found the strength to reach down inside myself, clear away the cobwebs and do what I needed to do.

For the last few months of my Sophomore year, I focused almost exclusively on my classes and before long, my grades were back up. When I applied for a transfer to Spelman for my junior year, I was accepted.

I felt an immense sense of pride. I'd been through the trenches, falling deep down into a hole of despair. And I managed to pull myself out of it, to save myself. And even though I'd lost my way for a little while, I was now back on track to fulfilling my dreams. I was finally going to Spelman. I wasn't sure if being there would rid me of the depression that followed me my entire life, but I knew it was at least where I wanted to be. And for now, that was enough.

That summer, I decided to head back to Mobile to live with my aunt so I could save some money before my move to Atlanta in the fall. One afternoon, I was at my sister Bridget's house, helping her pack up and move. For hours, we moved boxes and furniture, all the while cracking jokes, reminiscing, and sharing our hopes and dreams for the future.

We managed to pack up and move most of the house on our own, but there was a refrigerator that we couldn't lift, no matter how hard we tried. We looked at each other, wondering what to do. I'd noticed that one of her neighbors who lived across the street had been hanging around outside. He was tall, around 6'1, with dark skin and features, and obnoxiously pretty teeth. I asked Bridget if she knew him, and she said she didn't.

"Well," I asked her, "do you mind if I ask him to come help us? We aren't getting this thing out of here by ourselves."

"Go ahead," she shrugged. I ran across the street and asked the man if he'd mind giving us a hand carrying some furniture. He smiled and nodded.

As the three of us lugged the refrigerator around the corner, I watched him from the corner of my eye. He was lean but strong, and the muscles in his arms bulged subtly, delicately. When he smiled, his eyes creased and shone, and I couldn't help but smile too. I could tell by the way he looked at me that he was admiring me as well. I recognized the familiar glimmer of desire, the way he flexed his jaw to try and pull me in.

After getting the fridge to my aunt's house, we sat down on the front steps and talked. He told me his name was Jason and he was getting ready to live in the house across the street from Bridget's where I'd initially spotted him. It was a small and simple house, but his mom owned it and she was letting him live there rent-free. The conversation flowed so easily, and it felt like we'd known each other for years.

After that day, Jason and I began spending more and more time together. I could tell that he liked me, but I was hesitant to give in to his advances. I wanted to maintain a bit of mystery, to stretch and prolong his curiosity for as long as possible.

For weeks, he'd come by my aunt's house and we'd sit in the front living room talking. He was charming, almost alarmingly so, and I felt my defenses weaken the more time we spent together. Eventually, when he asked me out on a date, I yielded. My desire for him, to know him and be close to him, was greater than my need to remain an enigma. I wanted him to know me too. I wanted to let him in.

On our first date, we went to the movies together. I don't think I paid any attention to the screen the entire two hours, as I was so focused on how much I enjoyed the feeling of my hand in his. After the movie, we went to a fast food joint nearby and had burgers and fries. I didn't mind the low maintenance nature of the date, since I knew he didn't have much money.

After that, we became glued to each other. We'd spend long evenings sitting on the green sofa at my aunt's house, just talking about life. He was so ambitious, and intelligent in a way that excited me. He shared his dreams and desires, his aspirations for the future. He told me how he had been studying business at Tuskegee University, but he had to drop out since he didn't have the money to continue. Now, he was back home saving up so he could go back. I related to his story since it was so similar to my own.

He shared his ambitions with me, his wish to travel and see the world. I loved listening to him talk. I was so attracted to his determination to build a better life for himself. He'd come from nothing and he was hell-bent on changing his circumstances in life, on ensuring that his future family lived more comfortably than he had.

It wasn't long before we fell in love. I wanted to spend every second with him. I loved the way he laughed, and the confident way he walked, like every step he took was deliberate, was part of a greater purpose. We were both short on cash, saving up money to continue our studies, I at Spelman and he at Tuskegee. So we didn't go out much, and our time together consisted of us talking or hanging out at his house. After a few weeks, he asked me to move in with him and I agreed.

I knew it was fast, but I felt like I was grown, too grown to be living with my aunt. We were in love, and this is what people in love did. Plus, it was only a temporary situation. By the end of the summer, I'd be heading off to Atlanta. If we lived together, we could spend as much time with each other as possible.

We even got jobs together at a Winn Dixie that had just opened up down the street. I worked in the bakery and he was hired to bag groceries. Unfortunately, our employment there was short-lived. The store had brought on dozens of people in an initial hiring frenzy, but they slowly realized they'd taken on more hands than they needed and we were both laid off.

Despite the inconvenience of our unemployment, life still felt limitless. We were both en route to accomplishing our life dreams. And we were doing it together, in a sense. It truly felt like with him by my side, anything was possible. My feelings for him were intense and overwhelming. I'd never loved anyone this much. I wanted to drown in the affection I felt for him, to nuzzle into the crannies of my emotions and live there forever.

It was around this time, shortly after I was laid off from Winn Dixie, that I started feeling sick. Every morning, I'd wake up and vomit up the previous night's dinner. For days, I couldn't keep anything down. It didn't take me long to realize that my period was also late. I went to the grocery store and bought a pregnancy test, mostly to assuage my nerves. I was on birth control and every time we had sex, Jason wore a condom. We were always careful. But I had to be sure.

After taking the test, I sat on the toilet and waited for the results to appear. After five minutes, I looked down at the little white stick. Two bright lines stared up at me from the results screen. I blinked, willing one of them to disappear, praying with all of my might that my eyes were playing tricks on me. But the lines didn't budge. As I sat there, holding the positive pregnancy test in my hand like a stick of dynamite, tears rolled down my face. I was devastated.

I saw my dreams of attending Spelman, of finishing my degree, crumble before me. All the dreams that Jason and I had of the future, collapsed to the ground, disappearing in a flurry of dirt and dust.

I had to tell him, to share the news with someone, to say it out loud. I breathed deeply, trying not to cry. But I couldn't even get the words out. All I could do was lift the test so he could see what I was unable to say. He looked at the test, then at me, then back at the test. His mouth fell open and stayed like that, slightly agape, and his eyes widened. He was as shocked as I was. *How did this happen? We were so careful.* I shrugged, unable to respond. Did it even matter now? It had happened, and now we had to deal with it.

Before I had a chance to tell anyone in my family, Jason had run home and told his mom the news. I was annoyed, but I had bigger problems to worry about. I told my sister Bridget hoping she'd be able to tell me what to do. Within a day, the whole family knew. That's the beauty of having sisters, I suppose. News travels fast.

Within a few hours, they were all calling me, asking me what I was going to do. I could tell they were disappointed that I wouldn't be able to fulfill my goal of going to Spelman, but they never made me feel bad about my pregnancy. They assured me that whatever I decided to do, they'd be there for me. It was a difficult moment in my life, but I felt extremely grateful that I at least had a supportive and loving family behind me. And honestly, I didn't know what I was going to do.

I'd always dreamt of becoming a mother, of having children. But this wasn't how I wanted it to happen. I wanted to be established in my life, to have a job where I could support them. I wanted to be happily married. I wanted the nuclear family, the two-parent household – the thing I'd never had.

One day, a few days after discovering I was pregnant, Jason and I were sitting in our kitchen chatting. He looked at me, a serious, pensive expression on his face.

"Cathey," he said, the muscles in his jaw clenching, "do you want to get married?" He held out a ring, a simple silver band he'd gotten from his mother.

I looked at him hard, staring into his deep brown eyes. His face was expectant, almost desperate. I nodded.

"Yes," I said, holding out my hand. He slipped the ring onto my finger, and pulled me in close for a kiss. We smiled at each other, both of us a little confused and a little unsure if we were making the right decision. But I knew I loved him. And I didn't want to bring my child into an already broken family. I didn't want them to bounce around between their mother and father's separate houses. I wanted them to be raised in a home, with two parents and an endless supply of love. Our beginning wasn't perfect, but we could still make the most of it. We could still scrap together the good and build something worthwhile, a beautiful life. We had love, maybe that would be enough to carry us through.

I told my family and friends the news, and we immediately started planning my wedding. Like so many young girls, I'd always dreamt of my wedding day. My family wanted me to get married at our church in Coden, close to where I grew up, and I'd always imagined myself walking down the aisle there too.

I started buying bridal magazines and exploring color combinations, settling on peach and ivory. My cousins and sisters all offered to help me, all of us getting excited at the thought of a family wedding, the spirit of celebration lifting our spirits. My cousins planned a seafood buffet for after the ceremony, and I went to a shop to look at invitation cards.

At this same time, Jason's mother, who was fully aware that I was planning everything myself, took it upon herself to order invitations without telling us. They were totally wrong. They weren't the right colors, didn't follow the template I'd wanted and she even spelled my name wrong. I was furious. She, on the other hand, was adamant that I have my wedding in Mobile, insisting that she would not attend if I had it in Coden or Bayou La Batre.

Even though I'd always wanted a wedding, I called the whole thing off. I told Jason that I didn't want the wedding if that's how it was going to go, with his mother calling all of the shots. We wouldn't have a ceremony, we'd just be married by a Justice of the Peace. It wasn't what I wanted, but it was better than the alternative. My entrance into his family was already off to a rocky start, but I was determined to make things work.

On February 7, 1986, the day of our would-be wedding, I woke up and got ready to head over to the courthouse. I wore a knee-length wool blue skirt and a long-sleeved fuschia shirt with a ribbon in the front. Jason wore a white shirt and slacks, with a blue tie. Just as we were getting ready to leave the house, he told me that the plans had changed. Instead of going to the courthouse, as we'd agreed, we were going to his parents' house to get married.

I stopped, shocked that he'd arranged this without even consulting me. The whole thing had his mother's fingerprints all over it. I felt sick to my stomach. How could he do this to me? It was *my* wedding. I deserved to have a say, to decide where I'd be married and by whom. I couldn't put into words the hurt I felt.

Jason didn't seem to care about my concerns. It was no big deal, he insisted. It was just a small ceremony anyway. Reluctantly, we walked down the street to his family's home. We walked inside, to the back of the house, where his parents, sister and brother were waiting, as well as the pastor from their church.

I wanted to throw up. He had witnesses, and his family present. I had no one. I was alone. This wasn't how it was supposed to happen, this wasn't what I wanted. But what could I do now? Everyone was waiting for me, for us.

I was livid, and I did nothing to hide it. As we stood before the pastor, alarm bells went off in my head. "What have you done?" a little voice whispered. A life was stirring in my belly, but there was something else growing there too. A sinking feeling.

This was the beginning of my new life, as a wife and a mother. But somehow, it didn't feel that way. It felt like an ending, like a door was being slammed shut in my face. And there was nothing I could do but stand there, staring with wide eyes at a future I felt was decided for me.

CHAPTER 4

When The Truth Comes Knocking

When I became pregnant, something shifted inside of me, every cell of my body expanding to make room for the new life. And I don't just mean this in the physical sense. My thoughts and emotions were a garden of worries, fears, dreams and hopes, all of them preoccupied with the little bean growing inside me.

Jason and I had made many sacrifices to ensure our future family had it better than we both had growing up. After we got married, Jason enlisted in the military. It seemed like the best route for us to take at the time. We'd have guaranteed income, our housing and health insurance would be taken care of, and we could both go back to school. The only downside was that almost immediately after enlisting, he was deployed to Germany, which meant he'd be gone for most of my pregnancy and the birth of our child.

I'd never imagined that I'd spend my first pregnancy on my own, but I had to adjust rather quickly to our new reality. Still, every milestone that passed felt bittersweet; I didn't want to be experiencing all of these moments alone. The first time I felt the baby moving inside me. Discovering it was a boy. His first kick. The way his heartbeat progressed, getting stronger and more alive with every passing appointment.

This was a time before cell phones and video calls, so I couldn't just press a button on a screen and show Jason my growing belly or the ultrasound photos. He wasn't there when my hankering for oranges struck (my most unusual pregnancy craving), to help me peel and cut them open. He wasn't around to get me a pint of butter pecan ice cream at midnight or fix me a snack when I woke in the morning ravenous and grumpy. I couldn't even just call him when I wanted to.

In the past, I'd daydreamed about what it would be like the first time I got pregnant. In my fantasies, my husband and I would go to all of my doctor's appointments together, both of us tearing up when we heard our baby's heartbeat for the first time. We'd rub oil on my belly, laughing when I outgrew my favorite clothes. In none of my reveries was I navigating this beautiful but stressful phase of life on my own.

I was happy to at least have my family nearby. Before getting pregnant, I hadn't planned to stay in Mobile for so long, but I was grateful for it now. Many of my sisters had children of their own, so they helped answer many of the questions I had, eased my concerns and prepared me as best as they could.

August 3, 1987 began like so many others had at that time, except for one small detail. Soul food. I woke up that morning with an intense and desperate craving for salty pork chops, buttery cornbread, tender and garlicky green beans and sugary-sweet candied yams. After using all of my might to lift myself out of bed, I waddled over to the kitchen and spent the next few hours preparing a meal that took me straight back to my childhood.

After I finished eating, the itis hit me like a ton of bricks. About 30 minutes later, this intense pain in my stomach woke me up. I sat up on the couch, wondering if I'd overdone it with dinner. As I walked over to the bathroom, I felt something wet trickle down the side of my leg. Oh god, I said out loud to myself, it's happening, it's happening! My water just broke! For a second I just stood and stared at the small puddle on the ground near my feet. But the sharp pain ripping through my stomach quickly brought me back to reality. I ran to the telephone and called my sister Bridget, who lived nearby. She told me to get ready, she'd be right over to take me to the hospital. I called a few other family members as well as my mother-in-law and let them know I was going into labor.

I grabbed my overnight bag, which I had packed and prepped for this moment, and rummaged through it to make sure I hadn't forgotten anything. I couldn't believe it was finally time. My baby was on his way. I wished that Jason was near me, to hold my hand through the fear, and assure me that everything was going to be okay.

When Bridget and I arrived at the hospital, which was one of the newer and nicer facilities in Mobile, the nurses took me straight to my room where they checked my dilation. Thanks to Jason's health insurance, I had a private room that was equipped with everything they needed for the delivery. A little while later, my doctor came in to check on me. In Dr. Foster's presence, I instantly felt a rush of relief. He was average height, about 5'9, with a light complexion and kind, gentle eyes.

I'd known since the moment I discovered I was pregnant that I wanted as close to an all-Black healthcare team as possible. Even though I'd always prayed for the day I became a mother, there was still a part of me that was terrified that I might, like my own mom, die giving birth. Something about being surrounded by Black folks reassured me and cushioned me from my fears. If, God forbid, something did go wrong, they'd be more likely to help me. I'd done some research, and Dr. Foster seemed like a perfect fit for me. All my friends and family members who'd gone to him had received exceptional care. And I was also familiar with his family. I felt safe with him, like he genuinely saw me and listened to my concerns.

Unfortunately, I couldn't say the same for everyone. Right before my nurse came in to administer my epidural, my mother-in-law showed up in the delivery room. We didn't have the greatest relationship, but I didn't mind her being there. She was my son's grandmother after all. But I knew that once the baby was on his way out, I didn't want her in the room. As soon as the doctor told me it was time for me to start pushing, I shot my sister a loaded look. She nodded at me knowingly.

"Cathey doesn't want everyone in the room while she's in labor. I'll come out and let you know when the baby is here," Bridget told my mother-in-law, guiding her toward the door. My mother-in-law looked annoyed, shooting me a sideways glance over her shoulder as she left the room. A few minutes later, as I was in the middle of a push, she barged back in. And as if that wasn't bad enough, she had a camera with her too, and she was snapping pictures of me fully exposed. She didn't care about my boundaries or how violated it made me feel. I was livid with how bold she was being, taking advantage of me when I was in no position to do anything about it.

But my son was making his descent into the world, and I didn't have the time or energy to be worried about his grandmother. I looked back at Dr. Foster, who was positioned between my wide, open legs, instructing me when to push and when to breathe.

"Ok Cathey, I need you to give me one big push now," he said, his voice firm and commanding, but gentle. I closed my eyes, took in one big gulp of air, and pushed with everything I had, my jaw clenched and my hand squeezing Bridget's. I felt a pressure around my pelvis, and suddenly, in an instant, relief.

A minute later, Dr. Foster handed me my perfect baby boy, all 8 pounds and 21 inches of him. I held him in my arms for the first time, tears streaming down my face. As I lay there, exhausted and covered in various bodily fluids, I felt a degree of happiness I'd never felt before. I was overwhelmed and bursting with love, something even greater than that actually.

As I stared down at his tiny head resting on my chest, I knew that my life would never be the same again. *I* would never be the same. The moment he exited my body, this living, breathing piece of me, my world was forever altered, improved, and meaningful in a way it couldn't have been without him. I kissed his tiny head and whispered his name. DK.

A little while later, my mother-in-law came closer to meet her grandson. She picked him up, inspecting his face with an air of scrutiny and doubt. A scowl crossed her downturned face as she stared at my son.

"Mama's baby, daddy's maybe," she said, smirking in my direction. I stared back at her in disbelief, my jaw hanging at the ridiculous insinuation and her callous timing. Bridget, who was standing next to my bedside, stomped over and grabbed DK from her arms and handed him back to me. She looked ready to sock the bitter old woman, but Dr. Foster, accurately anticipating an escalation, intervened. "All right, I think Cathey needs some time to rest, folks," he said, stepping between the two of them. He looked at Bridget, nodding towards me. She huffed back to my bed and stood beside me.

For the next few hours, various family members poured into and out of my hospital room. My dad, the rest of my sisters, my aunts and cousins, all of them cooing over my child. "What a healthy and handsome boy!" they all squealed, caressing his cheeks and chubby little hands.

There were a few comments about the color of his ears, which I tried my best to ignore. My boy was barely 24 hours into life, and colorism had already crept its way in. My son was perfect, and I felt the urge to shield him from anyone who might imply otherwise.

After I gave birth, my sister Vee insisted I move in with her and her son, at least for a little while as I adjusted to the realities of being a new mother. I was reluctant at first, but it turned out to be the best thing I could have done. I was alone, and figuring out how to care for a baby was a terrifying endeavor. There was so much I didn't know, so many things I had to learn how to do on the fly: how to properly mix the baby formula, how to fill the water basin for his bath with the right amount of water at the correct temperature, how to swaddle him, how to hold him. The questions were endless.

I'd also read tons of horror stories about allowing babies to sleep on their stomachs, and how it heightened the risk of Sudden Infant Death Syndrome. For days I was paralyzed with paranoia, and I'd wake up in the middle of the night in a frenzy, certain that I'd accidentally put DK down in his crib on his stomach instead of on his back.

Thankfully Vee was there to walk me off the ledge, to ensure me that he was fine and reminding me to rest. When he's asleep, you should be asleep too, she'd reiterate every time she caught me watching over him in his cradle.

By the time I moved back home two months later, we'd settled into a good routine. DK was beginning to sleep through the night, and I felt confident in my ability to care for him.

When we were at home alone together, I spent so much time just staring at his tiny face in awe. His eyes, which looked so much like my own, looked back at me with a curiosity that made me want to cry. He had his dad's pouty lips and even though he was only a few months old, he was already tall for his age, something he'd also undoubtedly inherited from his dad's side of the family.

As I watched him with wonder and amazement, I'd also think of my mother. She'd given birth to nine children in her lifetime. And even though I could never ask her myself, I was confident that each time (except for my birth, of course), she'd felt this same joy I was now experiencing. She'd probably done the same things I was doing, gazing at the miracle of life we'd been gifted, at the little fingers and toes, the wide and inquisitive eyes. She probably felt the same protective spirit I was now feeling, the subtle but indubitable realization that I'd do anything in my power to shield him from harm. I never felt closer to my mother than when I became one myself.

My days passed in a sleepy but joyful haze. My sisters and other family members dropped in often to spend time with me and the baby. My friend Candace, the one who'd supported me through my depressive episode at Dillard, called me almost every day to check in and see how we were doing. We'd remained the best of friends even after I left New Orleans, and I'd asked her to be DK's godmother. She agreed and when she had a lull in schoolwork, she drove down to Mobile to spend a weekend with us.

Jason also called when he could. It was hard raising my son alone, without his father. But I knew he was experiencing his hardships too. Not only had he missed the birth of his son, but he never got to see him at all. When we spoke, I'd gush about the progress he was making, whether it was lifting his head or laughing, or how his face was beginning to change. And I could hear the sadness in Jason's voice, even if he never said it out loud or verbalized how he was feeling.

Fortunately, he wouldn't have to wait too much longer to meet his son. In December, when DK was four months old, we got the official orders permitting us to join Jason in Germany. I packed up our small house and all of our belongings and the two of us got ready to move across the world. I'd never even been outside the country, so the notion of living somewhere new was both terrifying and exciting. I hated the idea of being so far away from my community, from my sisters and friends. Who would I lean on for support? How would I make friends, seeing as I didn't speak German? Was I allowed to work? What did being a military wife even entail? I had so many questions rolling around in my mind, anxieties about a future where I had no idea what to expect.

But I tried not to dwell too much on the scary parts, and to lean into the adventure of it all instead. This was an experience of a lifetime. When I was a little girl, I dreamt of doing something like this, living in faraway places, traveling the world, and experiencing more of what this planet has to offer. Now, I was actually doing it. And I was doing it with my very own family.

In mid-December, after many tearful goodbyes, DK and I boarded a flight for Wildflecken, a district in central Germany where the American military had an army base. DK, who was fitted in a thick and fluffy white and yellow onesie with a hood, fussed and cried for a little while, but eventually, we both fell asleep. The flight was 12 hours long, so by the time we arrived, I was beyond ready to be off that plane. More importantly, I was ready to finally see Jason, after being apart for nearly a year.

As I pushed the stroller through the airport towards the arrivals gates, I looked around anxiously, searching for the familiar face of my husband. As soon as I spotted him, waiting for me with a big smile on his face, my worries melted away. He ran towards us, and I opened my arms for an embrace. For a minute, we just held each other. I hadn't realized how much I missed the way he smelled, the familiar and comforting cadence of his breath. I could have stayed in that moment forever.

After a minute, Jason bent his head down into the stroller to meet our son for the first time. DK looked up at him curiously through layers of clothing, their eyes meeting one another for the first time. I watched them as they watched each other, my heart melting into a pool in my stomach. Jason picked him up and hugged him, kissing his head and repeating 'Hi son,' over and over again.

It felt good to finally be together, as a family, to have a husband again. For the past five months, I'd felt like a single mother and I was happy to finally be sharing the responsibility of caring for our baby boy – or at least that's what I thought would happen.

Before arriving in Germany, I thought that he'd be working regular 8-5 hours. I'd kiss him and see him off in the morning, and he'd be back in time for dinner. But as I very quickly found out, that was far from the case.

Jason belonged to the army, to his unit. His hours were unpredictable and all-encompassing, and I never knew when he'd be coming home. He worked all hours of the day and night, and sometimes on weekends too. My son and I barely saw him. And I never got a break from taking care of DK. At least back home in Mobile, I had family and friends to help me out. But in Germany, I had no one. And the responsibility for taking care of our son rested solely on my shoulders. I didn't understand why I was spending hours waiting for him to come home, and he seemingly never came. And Jason never bothered to explain.

One evening not long after I'd arrived, I'd had enough. I was beyond exhausted and the baby had been fussing all day long. I was desperate for Jason to come home so I could have a little reprieve, just a little time to rest. Caring for a baby is a full-time job. I couldn't even look away for a second. I'm sure the 'baby blues' was intensifying my emotions, and heightening my response to Jason's absence. But whatever the cause, after hours of waiting, I packed up DK, hopped into my car, and drove to the army base.

I stomped into the building and marched right up to his unit, yelling his name. He walked up to me, his face terrified. I was blind with rage and exhaustion. "When are you coming home? I need a break from this baby. I'm so tired!" I screamed. I realized then that I was making a bit of a scene, but I didn't care. I'd never felt so unhinged in my life. And Jason sensed it too. He tried to comfort me, but at the same time, he knew he had to de-escalate the situation and fast. He pulled me to the side, away from the small crowd that had gathered to see what was going on.

"You can't be coming in here like this, Cathey," he said, his voice low but firm. He assured me that he'd come home soon, as quickly as he could, and pleaded with me to leave. I wasn't satisfied with his response, but I nodded my head and left.

Later on, Jason's commanding officer called him into his office and told him he'd better explain his job to me properly, and to not let my outburst happen again. That night, when Jason finally got home from work, he sat me down and explained everything. He told me that he was required to work extra, that this wasn't a conventional job and he didn't have conventional hours. He was a private first class, which was one of the lowest rankings in the military. This meant that when duty called, he had to answer. Unfortunately for me and DK, when it came to my husband's job, we had to play second fiddle.

I was more annoyed with him for not preparing me better than I was at his unreasonable hours. If he'd at least told me in advance what to expect, we could have avoided the entire ordeal. But I had come in blind and full of hope and misplaced expectations.

It's safe to say that I had a bit of a rough start, but things improved eventually. As time went by, I began to meet other wives, who, like me, had packed up their whole lives and families to be near their husbands. And I quickly learned that there was a professional and social order that couldn't be violated. The enlisted personnel, like Jason, were underneath the officers. And the two groups never mingled. That segregation extended to their families too. The wives of the enlisted personnel didn't socialize with the wives of the officers. I didn't mind at all, as I'd found decent camaraderie and support in my own little bubble.

But just as I was starting to get comfortable, learning the ropes, establishing a routine and making friends, the plans shifted. Jason was being transferred to Baumholder, a town near the border with France. So, just four months after arriving in Germany, we had to relocate once again, this time luckily just three hours away.

In Baumholder, we lived in a German community in military housing. There was another enlisted family around the same age as us from Georgia living in the unit below us, and they also had a young child. I developed a close bond with the woman and before long, our families were inseparable. When our husbands had time off, the six of us would travel together, taking road trips over the border to the Czech Republic to spend the day in Prague. I loved walking around the city's cobblestone streets, admiring the diverse architecture, the historic buildings and bridges. It was so unlike the towns and cities I'd known in the U.S., a stunning blend of old and new, history preserved in time. I felt like I'd been transported to a different world, like I was a character living in one of the many novels I'd read as a young girl.

We also spent a lot of time exploring Berlin – both before and after the fall of the Berlin Wall in 1989. We felt the crispy air of change around us as we walked through the city, a particular thickness in the wind that carried the inevitable. Armed guards strolled next to us, a subtle reminder of the specter of war which loomed like a shadow over everything. There was also the obvious reality that we were Black in a predominantly White country (and continent for that matter), one that often made no secret of its racism – or its fascination. The locals were enamored with our brown skin, and on more occasions than I can count, they'd reach out and touch DK's hair. I was irked each time and I wanted nothing more than to reach out and swat their hands away. But the sight of the German Polizei patrolling every corner deterred me. I just wanted to get back home without any incidents.

It wasn't all war and army boots though. In the winter, we'd drive around exploring the different Christmas villages and markets. Living in Germany, it was impossible to not be in the Christmas spirit. The streets, which were covered in snow, were all lit up with lights, and every storefront was decorated with nutcrackers and ornaments. It was like walking inside of a holiday movie. We'd sip mulled wine and snack on gingerbread, bratwurst sausages and stollen, a sweet, spiced bread filled with nuts and candied fruit. I'd watch DK's little face, all lit up by the lights, in the carrier on Jason's back.

Jason's brother was also stationed in Germany at the time, less than three hours away from where we were living in Fulda. He had a wife and two children, and we'd spend all of the holidays together. It was nice to have relatives nearby to create a little community in Germany, so far away from home.

It would have been easy during this time to feel like I was on an extended vacation, but I was barely ever idle. I worked various jobs, from hosting at the Officer's Club, an exclusive restaurant only for the officers (where I encountered innumerable disrespectful and flirtatious army personnel), managing a lunch food truck and retail at the Post Exchange. I still had ambitions to go back to school and get my degree, so I took night classes when I could.

It was a happy time for our family, and I loved that I was able to give my son this life and these experiences. He attended a German pre-kindergarten when he was three, and naturally, he began to pick up the language. He was the only American and the only African American in his school, and many of the army wives thought I was crazy for entrusting him to the care of 'those Germans,' as they so callously put it. But I knew there was an irreplaceable value in letting my son fully experience life in Germany. DK would benefit so much.

But in addition to experiences, I wanted to give him something more – a sibling. In our third year in Germany, we decided it was time to start trying for a second baby. I'd always known that I didn't want too large of an age gap between my children, and three to four years seemed like the right amount of time.

We tried for a few months, but nothing seemed to be happening. My doctor insisted it was because I'd been on birth control for so long and I just needed to be patient. Around this same time,

Jason was beginning to think of his future in the military and how he wanted to move forward. One option was to stay where he was, and gradually move his way up the ranks as an enlisted soldier. The other option was to apply for the Army's Green to Gold program. If he took this route, he would essentially be leaving active duty to finish his degree. After graduating, he'd return to the military as an Army Officer.

As an officer, he'd have more opportunities to do work he actually wanted to do, and importantly, he'd make more money. While he was in school, he would no longer be affiliated with the military. We'd lose our income and health insurance, and we wouldn't get to stay in military housing. This meant we'd both have to get jobs while he was in school, and we'd have to find a home on our own. It was a small sacrifice that would pay off in a big way in the long run. I was invested in the dream.

He applied, and a few months later, he got the news that he'd been accepted. I held a small party for him at our home, and his brother's family and all our friends came to celebrate with us. I made a big banner that read 'Congratulations, Jason!' and had gold bars on either side, signifying his journey towards becoming a Second Lieutenant. I hung it out on the stairs leading up to our apartment. This was a big deal. Jason would be the first member of his family to become an officer, and he'd finally get to return to his studies, something he'd wanted to do for years. I was so proud of him, for everything he'd been able to accomplish. Even though I'd had to put my dreams on the back burner for a long time, I didn't mind. At least one of us was getting to live out our dreams, and that seemed better than nothing. Plus, I was hopeful my time was coming. I'd get my opportunity to do the same.

Despite my excitement, I was also nervous, because the timing couldn't have been worse. Shortly after he got accepted into the program, I found out I was pregnant. We were moving back to the U.S. with a toddler and a baby on the way – without health insurance, without jobs and a home. I wasn't sure how we were going to figure everything out, but I knew we had to do it fast. *I* had to do it fast.

For the next few months, I worked on getting our lives in Germany packed up and ready to go while Jason wrapped up his job. It had been a very happy and exciting four years, but I was excited to go back home to Mobile, to see my family again. In the summer of 1991, we boarded a plane and flew back home to the U.S.

By the time we arrived back in Mobile, I was five months pregnant. We stayed with family for the first few weeks, until we found an apartment. And Jason and I quickly got to work finding jobs. He was hired in the supply department at a local hospital, and I got a job administering eye exams at an optometrist's office. At the same time, we both enrolled in a local university and began working to finish our respective degrees – mine, a BS in psychology, and Jason's a bachelor's degree in business.

At school, I felt awkward and out of place. Most of the other students were younger, and their entire lives revolved around their university experience. I, on the other hand, was

26, married, a mother, and very visibly pregnant. It was hard to relate to the other students, whose biggest concerns were upcoming finals or whether or not their crush liked them back. My stresses centered around feeding my child, making sure I was taking my prenatal vitamins and the health of my marriage.

At the time, we also had to resort to using food stamps since the money Jason and I were both making at our jobs was barely enough to keep us afloat. At first, I didn't feel too much shame in it. I, like any mother, would do anything I had to do to take care of my family. And I knew our current situation was temporary, that soon both my husband and I would graduate, get good jobs and we'd be back to living a comfortable life. Our situation was *temporary*.

But when I went into the government assistance office to apply and pick up my food stamps, or to get special supplements offered by the WIC program, I immediately felt the burn of the workers' eyes. They looked at me like I was nothing, like I was a piece of trash that had just blown in from the street. I could easily discern what they were thinking from the judgy looks on their faces, the way they scanned me up and down, their eyes lingering on my bulging belly. *Just another pregnant Black girl, coming to us for handouts.* I often left the office on the verge of angry tears, disgusted by how awful they'd made me – and undoubtedly so many others – feel. They don't know you, Cathey, I'd tell myself as I drove off. They don't know everything you're capable of, all of the things you're going to do with your life. These pep talks worked to calm me down, but the feelings of degradation returned whenever I had to go back.

And the embarrassment didn't stop there. When I went to the grocery store, I'd take a deep breath before entering to prepare myself for the humiliation I'd inevitably face when I pulled out the little booklet of stamps and saw the disapproving look on the cashier's face. I'd try not to look around, actively avoiding the judgemental looks of the other customers.

I felt at odds with myself, unable to come to terms with how I felt about the whole thing. On the one hand, I knew there was nothing shameful about needing to access government assistance. Our situation was precisely why food stamps existed in the first place. And I would never look down on any person who used these services to care for their families. But that awareness didn't do anything to lessen my humiliation.

Even though I'd been relatively poor for most of my life, I'd never had to engage with these systems before. And I was quickly realizing what a degrading experience it was to deal with.

Since moving back to Mobile, I had been struggling to readjust. Everything, from school to work to home felt awkward and uncomfortable. One of the only things that still gave me joy was seeing my son. When I wasn't at school or working, I wanted to spend as much time with DK as possible. My aunt Marguerite had graciously offered to take care of him while Jason and I worked and went to school. But every second I spent away from him, I missed him dearly.

Jason, on the other hand, seemed to be right in his element. Since returning to his hometown, he'd been spending more time than ever with his family and his old high school friends, including some ex-girlfriends, and less time with me and DK. Sometimes, when he'd return home after being away for a few hours, I'd ask him where he'd been. He'd smirk and tell me not to worry, he was just visiting his parents. Maybe it was a woman's intuition, but something in my gut just told me he was lying. On more than one occasion, someone would call the house and hang up as soon as I said hello.

I felt like since coming home, there had been a shift in our relationship. I didn't understand it, especially as I was pregnant with our second child. In my mind, we should have been in a state of bliss. He should have wanted to spend what little free time he had with me, and with our son. I tried to bring up my concerns to him but he was always very dismissive. He never acknowledged my worries and barely did anything to comfort me.

Even though I sensed something was off, and vocalized it a few times, I mostly ignored my instincts about my marriage. It wasn't that I didn't want to deal with it, but I was juggling so many responsibilities that I didn't have the time or energy to fixate on it. I was trying to be the best mom to DK, who was preparing to enter kindergarten, while also working, going to school, cooking dinner and keeping a clean house. If I allowed myself to dwell on Jason's distant behavior and lies, it would have immobilized me completely.

Being that I'm also a spiritual woman, I was weary about carrying too much negative energy in my mind and body while I was pregnant. I didn't want to do anything that might compromise my baby's safe passage into the world or make my pregnancy more difficult than it needed to be. I still had so many anxieties around childbirth, fears that I might share the same fate as my mother. What if I too was destined to leave the world the same way I came into it, wrapped up in the muck of tragedy?

What I needed to focus on was my birthing plan, and how to ensure everything went smoothly. This time around, we simply couldn't afford for anything to go wrong. When I was pregnant with DK, we had a great health insurance plan from Jason's job in the military. But because of the Green to Gold program, we no longer had those privileges. The health insurance we could afford now wasn't great – and I was stressed about something bad happening, and us being unable to afford my care.

It didn't help that every step along the way seemed laced with challenges and roadblocks. I was still committed to having a Black doctor, but now I had to look for one that was within my meager budget. When I did find one, I went to his office for my initial exam. As I lay down on the examining table waiting to be examined, the doctor's hands began moving to places of my body they had no business being. I didn't say anything, retreating into silence as I had when I was violated as a little girl. But as soon as I stepped foot out of his office, I nearly passed out in the hallway in a fit full of tears. I held onto the wall to steady myself and walked to my car, the tears still streaming like a deluge down my face.

When I finally got to my car, I found myself driving to Dr. Foster's office. He was my last-ditch hope. I didn't know where else to go, or what else to do. I cleaned up my face, trying to betray the reality of what I'd just experienced, and I walked into his office. But the sight of a packed waiting room nearly brought me to tears again. Thankfully, his office manager, who also happened to be his wife, agreed to fit me into his jam-packed schedule. I rehearsed what I would say as I sat there, but when he finally called me in, I could barely muster out the first few words before I broke down into tears. I told him everything, about us losing our health insurance, about the difficulty in finding an appropriate doctor I could afford, about the doctor who'd fondled me in his office. Dr. Foster looked horrified. He grabbed my hand and reassured me the best that he could, offering his disgust at what I'd experienced and his promise that he'd take me on as a patient again. A surge of relief coursed through me; it was like breathing again after being stuck in a burning building. I thanked him profusely.

This was one less thing I had to worry about. I took things as easy as I could for the weeks before I was due. I wanted to delay having my baby until January to avoid having their birthday overlap with my own, on December 26th, or Jason's on December 28. But when I woke up on the morning of December 27, I knew I was going into labor. Whether I was ready or not, my baby had no intention of staying put any longer.

When we arrived at the USA Health Children & Women's Hospital, which was a far cry from the hospital where DK was born, the nurses had me wait in a small hallway. The way they treated me was already so different than it had been the first time around, where they'd quickly wheeled me to my delivery room when I arrived.

As I waited on a chair in the narrow hall, my breathing getting more and more ragged with every painful contraction, Jason held my hand to try and calm me down. I'd asked when I could get something for the pain, but the nurses brushed me off and told me I had to wait. After sitting there for what felt like forever, I was finally given a bed. A nurse came into the room to check on me, and I asked her again when I was getting the epidural.

"Oh, it's too late for that now. You don't need an epidural anyway. You'll be okay," she said dismissively. I gasped, feeling both shocked and terrified. "But wait a minute," I told her, as she turned to leave. "I haven't done any Lamaze classes. I don't want a natural birth. I *need* an epidural." She shrugged and walked out of the room, dismissing me and the terrible pain that was coursing through me.

A little while later, Dr. Foster came in to check on me. I was experiencing the worst pain I'd ever felt in my life. My entire body from my waist down felt as though it was being torn apart with a hot iron. Dr. Foster tried to calm me down, to help me breathe through the contractions, but I was in so much pain I could barely hear what he was saying. By this point, the baby was coming, already pushing their way through my body, so it was far too late for an epidural.

As Dr. Foster prepped me to start pushing, the head nurse, the same one who denied me the epidural, was busy helping Jason put little blue booties on over his shoes. She was more concerned about covering up his shoes than she was about me, the patient, the person whose body was currently being torn open in the most traumatizing way. I snapped, my patience tearing at the seams as if in solidarity with my body. "Forget about the damn booties!" I yelled, both at Jason and the nurse.

Dr. Foster held my hand to try and bring my focus back to giving birth. By that point, I needed the baby out of me, fast. I didn't think my body could withstand the pain any longer. Finally, after 25 minutes of pushing, my beautiful baby girl was born at about 2:25 pm.

The nurse turned to me then. "See," she said smugly, "you didn't need the epidural." Before I could even respond, Dr. Foster jumped in to defend me. "Yes she did," he shot back, a sharp edge in his voice. He tried to hand the baby to me, but I was still in so much pain, I shook my head.

"No, Cathey," he said, holding this beautiful little infant in front of me. "Come on, hold your baby. Hold your baby." I took the baby into my arms, her little head resting on my chest. I was in so much agony, I could barely see straight. I felt like I'd been robbed of having a proper first introduction to my child. I wanted to be happy when my baby was born, glad to finally see her come into the world, not paralyzed from the trauma and pain I'd just experienced.

Eventually, I was able to greet my new baby, Ziiomi. My birthing experience with Zii made me think of my mom. It made me wonder if she'd experienced that same dismissal of her pain or if she'd had racist doctors who callously believed that Black women have a higher pain tolerance than women of other races. I, luckily, made it through to the other side of my suffering; my mom hadn't. I don't know the details of her death, but after having gone through such a traumatic birth myself, thanks to the cruelty of the medical staff, I felt like I somehow understood my mom a little better, as if our mutual suffering bonded us even through that wide gap of life and death.

The difference was I lived through it, and my daughter wasn't going to grow up without a mom. I was beyond thrilled to have a baby girl. Throughout my pregnancy, and after Zii's birth, I'd play Angie Stone and Joe's song *More Than a Woman*, over and over again, lingering over the lyrics 'a girl for you and a boy for me'. It was what I'd always wanted, and I felt deep down inside me that our family was now complete. I felt that having Zii was a blessing from God, like he was endowing me with the privilege and responsibility of mothering this little girl in all of the ways I'd always craved mothering. I had to make sure I did with her all of the things I'd wanted to do with my mother, but couldn't. It was as if I was getting a do-over of my childhood, that through mothering Zii, I would somehow also be mothering my own younger self.

I'd decided not to go back to school after giving birth, at least not right away. DK was in kindergarten at the time, and I didn't want to be leaving a newborn baby with Aunt Marguerite, who was by that time in her seventies. I didn't mind too much though, as it allowed me to spend time with my little one.

We spent the next two years in Mobile, and in that time, Jason finished his degree and returned to the military as an officer. When he went back, he received orders that he'd be stationed in Fort Riley, Kansas. We'd decided that Jason would go first, to get us a house and get things ready, then me and our two kids would follow behind.

I didn't mind moving, and I was happy to be leaving Mobile, where Jason seemed to be enmeshed with his high school friends and life. I figured a move would be good for our family. I applied to continue my degree at Kansas State University, and I was accepted. I was intent on finishing school and proving myself, no matter how long it took. I wasn't going to let the fact that I became a mother at 21 stand in the way of my goals. Plus, being educated would only benefit my family. Without an education, I wouldn't be able to support my family, should something happen to Jason.

In 1993, six months after Jason moved, me and the kids headed to our new home in Fort Riley. We settled in pretty quickly and began establishing our lives. DK was in the second grade and Zii was almost two. This time around, I felt much more comfortable being back at school. Even though I was now even older than most of the population, I seemed to have regained some of my confidence. I had pledged Alpha Kappa Alpha Sorority when I was back in Mobile and quickly became involved with my local chapter in Kansas. Jason pledged Alpha Phi Alpha and also got involved with the community. Pretty soon, we'd found our own little family in Fort Riley. I got very close to my sorority sisters, many of whom also had husbands who were in the military. It was nice to have girlfriends who could so closely relate to my experiences as an army wife. Jason bonded with his Fraternity brothers, as well as the many Black officers he worked with. This vast group of friends became our community, the people we spent all of our time with and leaned on for support.

On the weekends, we'd have BBQs and dinner parties, our kids all becoming fast friends. By now, I understood the particular responsibilities that come with being married to someone in the military, especially an officer. I attended meetings for the wives of officers and got heavily involved in the activities on base. We attended military balls, holiday functions, promotion and retirement parties. As my husband moved higher up the ranks, I supported him along the way.

The men Jason was spending so much time with now were a huge improvement from the ones he'd been hanging around with back home. They were all successful, God-fearing men who loved and valued their families. I was hopeful that Jason would be inspired by them, to learn from the example they were setting that family came first.

In December of 1994, just a week before Christmas, my own family suffered an unfathomable loss. That week, my sister Genevieve called me on the phone. I answered her with a cheerful "Hi, sis!", but I quickly reeled it in when I heard the nervous quiver in her voice. "Cathey," she said through tears, "I don't know how to say this. Daddy... He's dead." For a moment, my mind couldn't quite process the words, and they sat in my mind as if floating on top of a murky pond, barely grazing the surface below. After a few minutes had passed, the weight of what she'd said hit me. *Daddy was dead.* I'd never see him again, never speak with him again.

He'd had a stroke a few years prior which rendered him noncommutative. My sisters, who were closer in proximity than I was, had cared for him during that time. I, on the other hand, only saw him a handful of times when we went home for the holidays.

Not long after, we were in the car making the long drive over from Kansas to Alabama. I was on my period (which has always been on the extreme side for me, with excessive bleeding and severe, debilitating cramps), was anemic and deeply emotional. The combination made me light-headed and dizzy, and I had to keep my head nearly outside the car window for the entire trip.

The loss of my father numbed me. I felt cold and empty, and there was a massive void inside of me that I realized would never be filled. There were so many questions I'd wanted to ask him about my mother, things only he would know. But now those questions were buried beneath the earth. Mom would remain elusive to me for the rest of my life, a reality that made me feel sick to my stomach. I'd officially lost both of my parents. I was one of those people now, the ones you feel a pinch of sadness for when you hear that their parents are both dead, saying to yourself, 'I'm so happy that's not me.'

After my dad's death, I clung even more desperately to my own family. I'd hoped that the new life we were building in Fort Riley would narrow the gap that I had felt between Jason and I in our marriage. We had a family, two beautiful children. We were building a life to be proud of. Why would he want to ruin that, to undermine the life we'd successfully built for ourselves, because of a wandering eye?

I placed that hope high up on the shelf of my awareness, above everything else. I told myself that he would be faithful and I went on with my life. I was committed to the idea of being a supportive officer's wife. I worked my butt off at school, throwing myself into my studies to distract me from something I felt but couldn't prove, and in my new job as a paraprofessional. And I tried to be the best mother I could be to my children, making them the center of my life. Between breakfast, school drop offs, studying, going to class, working, picking the kids up, making dinner, cleaning the house and putting everyone to bed, I had very little time to focus on anything else.

But a woman's intuition always finds its way to the fore. It slips through the cracks and crevices in your consciousness, sneaking up when it thinks you're not paying attention. It refuses to be ignored. I knew my husband was being pulled away from the marriage, but because I didn't have any proof, I felt helpless to do anything about it.

As it turned out, I didn't have to. One evening in 1996, just as I was clearing plates and pots from the table after dinner, Jason looked up at me from his chair and told me we needed to talk. I listened for DK and Zii, who were off in another room doing their homework, then nodded and sat down next to him. He told me that he had a new assignment in Korea, and he'd be going alone.

I was shocked, but I stayed silent, listening as he explained all of the reasons why he thought it was a good idea. I knew that he didn't have to go on a solo tour. If he wanted to do a tour of Korea, we could go with him. The military would easily and happily accommodate that. He didn't need to go to Korea at all. He was doing well in his career, and this would do very little to advance him further. I tried to ask him questions, to suss out his true intentions. I even brought up our children. DK was in the fourth grade and Zii was in kindergarten. They were so young, they needed their father. And a year was such a long time to be apart, for me to be raising our kids on my own. But it was obvious from his demeanor and the finality of his words that he wasn't asking for my opinion. He was just *letting me know* that he'd made this decision, and now our family would have to accept it. Again, on the list of priorities I was nowhere to be found.

I wasn't the only one confused by Jason's actions. His officer friends and fraternity brothers also questioned why he was going. "Are you sure you want to do this, man?" I'd hear them ask, gently. "You have a wife. You have two kids. Are you sure this is the right decision?" I could see the looks on their faces, the way they were quietly inspecting him, wondering what was going through his head. And I felt embarrassment, for both myself and for Jason. Nonetheless, my husband had made up his mind, and no amount of questioning was going to sway him.

Despite my bewilderment, I put on a happy front. I organized a going away dinner for Jason and invited all of our friends. I put on a beautiful dress and smiled through the evening, acting as if his decision to go was something we'd both wanted, something we'd decided together. But I could see very clearly that I wasn't fooling anyone. They were all watching us with curiosity, wondering, rightfully, how Jason could just pick up and leave his family like this. My sorority sisters were all married to military men. And his friends were officers, like him, many of them in even higher ranks. None of them would ever even imagine making a move like this without their families.

Instead of wallowing in my worries, I decided to try and get ahead of things, to try and figure out how to set our family up for success once Jason returned. I realized that when he came back from his tour, we'd probably have military orders as to his next duty station as he'd finished his job in Fort Riley. Before Jason left for Korea, I asked him to find out where he'd be stationed next, that way I could move there with the kids before he returned and get our life set up. I'd find us a house, get a job, get the kids into their new school. I didn't want to sit around and wait for him to get back before I could start living my life the way I wanted to. I was finally graduating that year and getting my degree after so many years of starting and stopping, of sacrificing my education. I was ready to start a career and flex my professional muscles.

A few months into his tour in Korea, he told me he was going to be stationed in Fort Stewart, Georgia, an army post south of Savannah. I quickly got to work planning our move. After Jason left, his fraternity brothers continued to check up on me and the kids. They'd drop by the house to take DK and Zii to the park down the street, giving me a break from being a full-time mother and father. And when it was time to make the move, at the tail end of 1996, they helped me prepare the house for the movers and to clean after they'd left. The military takes care of the entire moving process, packing you up and unpacking you at your next destination. I didn't think I'd miss much about Kansas, the cold, snowy winters and the dismal Black culture, but I would surely miss the people – our people.

Even when me and the kids moved to Georgia, our friends in Kansas continued to check up on us. At first, the calls were mostly routine, filled with questions about our new house and neighborhood, making sure we were safe, happy and healthy. But gradually, the conversations shifted.

One evening, around three months after the move, I was sitting on the couch resting when one of my sorority sisters called. The conversation was casual, and she asked me how the kids were doing and if I needed anything. But I could sense from the tension in her voice that something was off. "Cathey," she said, her voice low and heavy, "I don't want to upset you, but I need to let you know. We've been hearing things about Jason, about what he's doing out there in Korea." She went on to tell me that some people had seen my husband running around with another woman. Apparently, he's acting like he's not even married.

I felt like I'd just been punched in the gut. My stomach turned, and I suppressed the urge to vomit. I put my hand over my mouth to silence the scream I felt bubbling up. For a minute, I just sat in silence, waiting for the room to stop spinning, for my breath to catch and for the nausea to pass.

"Cathey? Are you still there?" my sorority sister asked, the concern in her voice rising. I had to get it together. What I wanted to do at that moment was scream that she was lying, trying to break up my family. I didn't believe that, of course, but I had to place my anger somewhere and that seemed less damaging to my life than believing that my husband was cheating on me.

"Yeah, I'm here," I responded, steadying my voice. I told her that what she'd heard was just a rumor, probably spread by some jealous, ill-intentioned person. "It's not true, girl," I said, attempting to sound light. "You know it's not true. You know our family, how happy we are." She tried to persuade me, to make me see that it wasn't just a rumor, but I shut the conversation down and hung up. After I got off the phone, I sat there, just breathing, listening to the voices of my kids laughing in the next room.

Could it be true? Was Jason cheating on me? I let the question linger in my head for just a second before I quickly pushed it away. Surely these were just rumors, I told myself. There's nothing to worry about.

That was how I carried on. And the truth was, I had so much to do in Fort Stewart. I had to teach my kids the ins and outs of our new neighborhood, where to catch the bus for school, find us a new church to attend, and go to PTA meetings. The list was endless. Plus, I had just gotten a new job I was very excited about. Blue Cross Blue Shield of Alabama had just opened a new branch in Savannah, and I was hired as an HR Specialist. I finally had a job I was proud of, one I was actually excited to go to every day.

I loved the routine of waking up every morning and getting all dressed up, applying my make-up, and putting on a nice pair of heels. I even loved the drive to Savannah and my tiny little cubicle. For once, I had something in life that was mine and mine alone. I'd sacrificed my own goals for so long to make sure Jason could achieve his. Now it was my turn.

Life felt like it was falling into place. My kids were healthy and safe, and they went to a good school that they liked. I was absolutely killing it at work, finally bringing in some decent money of my own. I'd even recommended some changes to our workflow and had them not only acknowledged by my superiors but implemented as well. I was making a name for myself professionally. I felt like I was finally being seen.

But every time I began to feel a little too content with how my life was going, reality came knocking on my door. I was getting calls regularly from my sorority sisters and frat brothers in Kansas, telling me about the stories they were hearing about Jason. He was out and about with another woman. He wasn't even trying to hide it, flaunting his infidelity around like it was something to be proud of.

Any time my friends would call me, begging me to believe them, I'd go straight into denial mode. As they tried to convince me that it wasn't just a rumor, that I was too smart to believe that, I'd push right back, insisting they were the ones being naive. "Don't believe everything you hear," I'd snap at them. "I know my husband better than any of you!"

It was an exhausting cycle, and I wasn't convincing anyone, not even myself. If it was true, if Jason was cheating on me in Korea, what was I supposed to do? I hardly ever let myself go there because I wasn't able to face the daunting reality of what that would mean. But there were tiny pockets in time when the kids were fast asleep and the house was still and quiet, I'd lie awake in bed and let the questions linger. *Is Jason cheating? Do I stay, for the sake of the children? Do I leave, for the sake of the children? How do I move on from this?*

I never had any answers to these questions. And in all honesty, I didn't want answers. I just wanted the whole thing to go away. I'd given so much of my life to Jason. I'd traveled halfway across the world, and all over the U.S., just to help him chase his dreams. I hadn't only put my ambitions on hold for him, I'd changed so much of what I wanted just to accommodate him in my visions for my future. I needed this nightmare to end already.

Near the end of his tour, probably one month before he was due to return home, I finally worked up the nerve to ask. He'd called me to check in on the kids, to see how we were doing and I broke down, unloading all of the questions that had been rolling around in my mind. I told him that I'd been getting phone calls and hearing rumors that he was being unfaithful to me. I'd defended him for as long as I could, but now I needed answers. I needed him to tell me the truth.

He chuckled, and I could tell by the shuffling noises that he was shaking his head. He assured me that he wasn't doing anything wrong, that he would never betray me like that. Plus, he insisted, none of those people calling you are over here, they don't know what they're talking about. He told me that he loved me, that I was the only woman he wanted. I had been with him long enough to know his mannerisms and to detect when he was lying, but I didn't want to believe that was true. I decided to just put my concerns on the back burner until he got home. We wouldn't figure anything out while we were separated by so much distance.

But when he got back, somehow things managed to get worse. Instead of us feeling closer, somehow we felt even further apart. He was physically with us, but mentally and emotionally, he was distant, detached from me and the kids, his mind elsewhere. And soon enough, even the physical proximity became shoddy.

One Friday afternoon, Jason came home from work and began packing a bag. I watched him with curiosity, not saying a word. Finally, he turned to me and told me that he was going to Columbus for the weekend to visit a friend. Columbus was a four-hour drive from Fort Stewart, and he'd never mentioned having any friends who lived there.

I was startled and asked him a barrage of questions. Who is this friend? Why haven't you ever mentioned him before? Did you go to high school with him? College?

"You don't know all of my friends, Cathey," he said, with a cold, callous indifference. I couldn't understand how he could just spontaneously drop this on me and expect me to be okay with it, especially since he'd recently returned from being away for a whole year.

This was quickly becoming Jason's modus operandi. He'd decide that he wanted to do something, without ever consulting with me, and I'd just have to go along with it. And perhaps in some way, I was complicit, because I did go along. I let him go, not feeling like there was anything else I could do. It's just one weekend, I told myself.

But it wasn't just one weekend. Pretty soon, it was three weekends out of every month. It became such a frequent occurrence that when Friday rolled around, my kids would already know the drill. "Are you leaving us again, Daddy?" they'd ask when they saw him standing by the door, his backpack by his feet. "Who is your friend, Dad? Can we go with you? Can we meet your friend too?"

My children missed their dad and it broke my heart to see how little he seemed to care. When he was away on these weekend trips, I was an emotional mess. I was more sure than ever that he was being unfaithful, no longer in denial about what was happening. Now, I was stewing in my fury. Was this person he was going to see in Columbus the same one he'd been seeing in Korea? Had they met years before through the military and had they been in communication all along? Did he plan that solo trip to Korea to be with her for an entire year? I know there was another military base in Fort Benning, near Columbus. Was that where she was stationed now? As the questions piled up in my mind, I began putting the pieces together.

I felt myself crumbling from the weight of it all. Luckily, as if sent by God to help carry me through this difficult time, I found a church home. The pastor and his wife, who were a young, fun couple with six kids, quickly welcomed us into the fold and within no time, we became a part of their extended family.

Outside of church, we would spend time with them, and my kids each had more than one best friend to play with. I confided in them both about what was happening in my marriage, something I usually wouldn't do because I was such a private person. But something about their demeanor comforted me and made me feel safe opening up. They consoled me and on many occasions, we even prayed together. Whenever Jason would attend service, they greeted him with love, showing no judgment. Attending church together was something I always wanted for my family because that's what I saw growing up. Although Jason rarely attended with us, I needed this grounding in my life so the kids and I made our way Sunday after Sunday.

At the same time, I began plotting my exit, imagining life as a single mom. What would it take? Should I move to Savannah, to be closer to my job? Did I have enough resources to support my children? I'd been doing so well at work and had been promoted several times since beginning my job. I'd also recently been accepted to the company's management training program, which would allow me to advance significantly in my career.

Professionally, I was thriving. Emotionally and personally, I was falling apart. I didn't want to be a single mom. I didn't want a divorce. But my marriage had deteriorated so severely over the past three years and I didn't know how we would ever repair things. It didn't help that Jason only ever seemed to dismiss my feelings, to deny that he was doing anything wrong. How could we even begin to fix our relationship if we couldn't acknowledge the massive wedge that existed between us?

Well, Jason had been coming up with some ideas of his own at the time. He came to me one evening after work as I was making dinner and told me he wanted to talk. By now, I'd surmised that whenever Jason approached me this way, it was because he'd come to some decision and our lives were about to change yet again. As I stood over the counter, chopping a head of lettuce, he told me that he'd been doing a lot of thinking lately, and had been reflecting on his goals and ambitions. In all of his reflection, he'd realized that he didn't want to be connected to the military anymore. He wanted to get out, to do something else.

I set down the knife, wiped my hands on a towel and turned to face him. He continued, explaining that he'd met some recruiters who specifically worked with Army officers looking to leave service, and they were willing to help him find something new. They'd get him connected to different job fairs, support him in interviews, anything it took.

"Well, what about my job?" I asked. I had been accepted into the management training program, which was a huge opportunity. I wasn't ready to just pick up and leave. He paused, considering his words. He told me the recruiters could help me find something new too. I sighed, exasperated by this new development. Sensing that I wouldn't just get on board with his plans this time, he moved in closer.

"Listen," he said, pulling me near him. "I know things haven't been great between us lately. But this is an opportunity for us to have a fresh start. *Our family* can have a fresh start." He painted a picture for me of the future, of how different our lives could be. We didn't need to keep living in this strange, tense limbo. The only way to escape our current conditions, to heal our family and our marriage, was to press the reset button. He'd do better and be more present in our lives. This was an opportunity for all of us, not just him.

I felt something stir inside me. It felt like hope. I'd been praying for a miracle for so long, and this sounded like the answer. I didn't fully believe or trust what he was saying, but I wanted nothing more than to keep my family together. I knew I'd have to sacrifice all of the hard work I'd put in at work, to give up the opportunities I'd busted my ass for. But wasn't it worth it if it meant that my family had a fighting chance?

I looked up at him, at the face I'd fallen madly in love with all of those years ago. By now, we'd been together for more than a decade. We had two beautiful children and a family that was worth fighting for. Despite the turbulence I'd experienced recently, I still loved him.

I imagined our family, all four of us together, bathed in the glow of happiness. I still had a vision of what our family could be, of how happy Jason and I could be together. I wasn't ready to discard that dream just yet, not if there was still a chance we could make it come true. I silenced the doubts raging in my mind and ignored the anxious flutter in my belly. I didn't know where this path would lead, but I was ready to follow Jason wherever he took us.

I held his face in my hands and kissed him softly. Then I nodded my head. "Okay," I said softly, a small smile crossing my lips. "Let's do it."

CHAPTER 5
Darkest Before the Dawn

I've always been a forgiving woman. I believe deeply in the healing power of mercy, and in every person's innate ability to transform themselves, to change and become better. So when Jason told me he was dedicated to the survival of our marriage, and that he wanted to work on us, I felt that I owed him the opportunity to do just that, to show me that he was capable of being the man I desperately wanted him to be. Despite everything he put me through, I still felt pangs of deep, debilitating affection towards him. I felt that if he could just prioritize our family over his own greedy, lustful desires, we could truly be happy together again.

I also felt an obligation to my children to stay. I did not want to be the reason for the demise of our family, a source of pain for them. For my entire childhood, I'd fantasized about one day having a family like the one I now had (of course, in those daydreams my husband wasn't cheating on me and I wasn't forced to sacrifice my aspirations at every turn to be with him). I wasn't ready to give up the potential we still had to be a united unit – a picture-perfect depiction of happiness.

I was convinced that I just had to hold out hope a little bit longer.

After Jason decided that he wanted to leave active duty and pursue a civilian career, he began working with recruiters to help him find a new job. Within a few weeks, he'd secured work in the finance department at the GE plant in Ringgold, a small town on the northern tip of the state of Georgia. Once again, we packed up our home and our kids and we moved. The area was mostly white, and I felt severely out of place. We were so far removed from our friends and families, from any sense of community. But it was just another small price to pay, I told myself. Better to be here together than apart somewhere else. I tried to make the best of it.

Over the next few months, I was the doting, supportive wife Jason wanted me to be. I got DK and Zii into school. I set up our new house, trying to make it as comfortable and homey for everyone as possible. I even found a new job working in the HR department at a manufacturing company in Charleston, Tennessee, about 50 minutes north of Ringgold.

As much as I wanted to be excited about all of these big changes, both my new job and our new town quickly made it clear that racism was alive and well. At my job, where I was the first Black person to ever work in a managerial position, I heard some of the White workers refer to me as 'that colored girl.' Obviously, I was upset. I approached the leadership team, expecting them to address the issue. But instead, they told me that I was overreacting. I wanted to scream, to throw things and tear down the entire place. Did they expect me to smile passively as their employees disrespected and belittled me to my face? No one else would ever have that kind of dehumanization projected onto them. But when I continued to voice my discomfort, they simply reminded me where I was.

"Cathey, this ain't New York. It's Tennessee," my boss said. Her point? People out here hadn't changed yet and they weren't about to. Whether I accepted it or not, this was the reality of living in a small town in the American South.

Life for my children at their school in Ringgold had its own set of challenges, which I was less willing to stay quiet about. At this time, DK was entering the 7th grade and Zii the 3rd. They took the bus to school, which would pick them up right outside of our house. One afternoon, a few months into our move, I noticed that Zii was coming home with really dirty clothes – something that was out of character for my tidy little girl. I asked her about it and she told me that the driver was making her sit on the floor of the school bus every day, as they refused to get the other kids to scoot over and make space for her. Her words made me dizzy as I recalled my own experience around that same age. I remembered how small I felt when I realized that people would treat me differently because of my race. I hated that the world had barely pushed forward since then, that nearly 30 years later the reality I lived, was as real and as biting for my children too.

I went straight into protective mama mode; there was no way they were going to belittle my child like that, not on my watch.

For the entire first semester, I made regular trips to the school to complain, wrote dozens of letters to the school board, and called them incessantly. I did everything I could think of. After Christmas break, when Zii got on the school bus, the driver announced to the other kids that they had to make space because 'somebody's parents had gone to the school board.' DK went through his own negative experiences both at the school and on the bus too.

The summer he was to enter 8th grade, he, like most boys his age, had a massive growth spurt. We were in the kitchen one day and I turned around and my once chubby little boy had grown overnight into this slim, lanky kid who was now towering over my 5'6 frame.

"Who are you?" I squealed, gesturing at his height.

Well, I wasn't the only one who noticed his growth. On his first day back at school, the bus driver, the same one who'd made Zii sit on the floor, looked him up and down, sneeringly.

"You think you're the big man on campus now, huh!" he snorted in a mocking tone, rolling his eyes.

After the first year, I realized that I could not allow my kids to stay enmeshed in such a racist and hateful county for school. I would have rather they didn't go to school at all than suffer at the hands of other people's ignorance. I found schools for them 15 minutes across the state line in Chattanooga. After some research, I realized those schools, though close by, had completely different demographics. There was more diversity and more opportunities for them to thrive.

After the move, our life in Ringgold became a bit more enjoyable. We still dealt with racism, but I paid it less mind. My kids were enrolled in extracurriculars – sports, dance, band, etc. Plus they'd started to make more friends and now there were playdates and sleepovers and birthday parties to attend. My kids settled very easily into their new routines. Our family joined a new church and even a bible study group. Even though I was constantly shuffling back and forth for all their activities, I didn't mind. I was happy for them to be outside of the house, away from the tension bubbling up between Jason and I – though they didn't escape completely unscathed. At one point, after Jason stopped coming to church with the kids and I, DK told me he wanted to stop going too.

"Why do I have to go if Dad isn't going?" he muttered. His words stung, and I tried to respond with patience, to not reveal my bitterness at his father.

"Everyone has to be accountable for the choices they make here on earth, DK. Let's just pray that one day, he'll join us again," I said, patting him gently on the arm.

From the outside, we were a picture perfect family. In reality, my marriage was in shambles. There were moments of love between us, times when he was so gentle and nurturing, that it was hard to believe he was the same man who was hurting me. But those times never lasted very long. I was doing everything in my power to bring a sense of harmony and love to the household, to turn the way we looked into what we actually were. Despite my best efforts, it was an impossible task to fulfill. With every step I took toward healing our marriage, Jason took one in the opposite direction. As determined as I was to fix things, he seemed equally intent on destroying them.

Even though I looked fine from the outside, I wasn't doing well, a fact my doctor pointed out to me during a routine check-up. I was either not sleeping at all, or sleeping far too much. I had no appetite. Truthfully, I felt hopeless, but I could never admit it. I couldn't face the fact I was sad. It helped that I hid it well. At least that's what I thought. My doctor told me he was going to write me a prescription for an antidepressant. I stared back at him, confused. "But I'm not depressed," I said, nearly choking on the last word. He gave me a slight smile.

"There's no shame in it, Cathey. Sometimes we just need a little help," he said, handing me the prescription. I took it, staring down at the messy writing. I made out a name: Buspar. As I left the office, I considered just throwing out the prescription, but without thinking, I ended up outside the pharmacy. Maybe my doctor was right. It couldn't hurt to just try. Anything was better than living with this impenetrable sadness, this doomed feeling that nibbled on the inside of my belly at all times.

A week or so later, Jason noticed the bottle. He picked it up, inspecting the little white pills inside, reading the label with a sharp attentiveness.

"What's this for?" he asked, shaking the bottle. I gulped.

"It's an antidepressant." He looked at me, something sharp and piercing in his gaze, but stayed silent. But after that, anytime we'd argue, he'd weaponize this knowledge he had, bringing up the fact I took antidepressants like it was a crime I committed, like he wasn't the reason I was depressed. All he had to do was change his behavior, but it seemed that was asking far too much.

Instead, he'd just try to 'buy' my forgiveness (without ever asking for it, of course, as that would require him to own up to his infidelity). One Christmas, he handed me a long, painfully soft mink coat. "Merry Christmas, dear," he said, draping it over my shoulders and kissing me on the side of my head. I ran my fingers through the fur, feeling down the sides. I walked to the mirror, inspecting my reflection. The coat was beautiful, and in it, I looked spectacular. But the coat reeked of Jason's lies, a reality that cheapened the luxury. I just wanted loyalty, but that was the one gift he was unwilling to give me. After he gave me the present, he snuck away to call his girlfriend.

Our relationship continued to deteriorate. I was lying in bed early one morning while the rest of my family slept. I loved this part of the day, when the house was silent, and a golden stream of light filtered in from the window near our bed. In these quiet moments, I allowed myself to feel hopeful, to imagine a different life. I closed my eyes, trying to breathe in the last few minutes of calm before the house sprang into action. I felt Jason stir next to me. It was far too early for him to be up for work, I thought to myself. He slowly and cautiously lifted himself out of the bed and tiptoed out of the room. I listened for his footsteps, curious as to what he was doing. As quietly as possible, I got up and followed him. He'd gone to our computer room in the loft upstairs

I stood outside the room for a moment before slowly creeping back to our room to start getting ready for work. But over the next few days, I noticed him repeating the same trek, early every morning while he thought I was still asleep.

My mind was reeling. What could he be up to? Was it porn? Gambling? A shopping addiction? I tried to keep myself from spiraling, at least not until I had concrete proof. One morning, after the kids had gone to school and Jason to work, I went back to the computer room. I sat in front of it for a moment, just breathing, steadying myself for what I might find. I clicked open the internet and checked the history. Jason wasn't so savvy, or perhaps he just didn't care, I'm not sure. But everything he'd done was there wide open for me to see. I opened his email, which he'd also left logged in and scrolled through the messages. I kept seeing one name come up, over and over again: Beverly. I opened an email from her and read through their long thread.

All of the pieces came together. Beverly lived in Wetumpka, Alabama and had been in the military. This was the 'friend' he was driving to Columbus to see every weekend when we lived in Hinesville. She was also in Korea, while he was on his single-man tour of duty.

My stomach turned. Here I was, quitting a job I loved and moving my kids to this backwoods town in the middle of nowhere for this man after he'd promised me he'd be better. And everything was the same as it always had been. When he came home later that night, I confronted him about it. He chuckled, his eyes inspecting me from head to toe.

"What, are you spying on me now?" he spat with a look of disgust on his face. "You need to stop snooping and mind your own business." I felt a surge of rage, a wave of hurt and anger building up inside me. He was cheating, but I was the one out of line for reading his emails without his permission? If it wasn't so infuriating, I would have laughed.

"Are you serious, Jason?" I shot back, stepping in front of him as he tried to walk away. "After moving us all out here, you're doing this to us?" He laughed dismissively. He looked at me, a sharp bitterness etched into his face.

"Look at this beautiful house you have," he said, raising his arms beside him as if in prayer. It was clear he thought I should just be grateful, to turn a blind eye to his infidelity because he was providing, as any man should for his family. I scowled at him, ready to strike back.

"Listen, I don't know what you think is happening, but I'm not doing anything," he said. He turned his back to leave but paused and looked at me again. "Even if I was cheating, what are you going to do, Cathey? Leave me? Come on now. Look at you. You're a grown woman with two kids and nothing to show for yourself. You need to drug yourself just to get through the day." I gulped back the lump that had formed in my throat. Don't cry, don't cry, don't cry, I repeated to myself. I wouldn't give him the satisfaction of a single tear, not now. He walked away while I stood there, breathing deeply.

We had some derivative of that same fight at least once a week, me pouring out my heart at Jason's feet, begging him to be better, and him brushing me off. Eventually, he started taking his weekend trips again, to visit his 'friend'— even as I pleaded with him not to go. And she began calling the house as well.

At first, she'd just call and hang up. But one day, she grew bold enough to ask to speak with Jason. I asked who I was speaking with, she chuckled and told me not to worry, Jason would know. I screamed at her to stay away from my husband, calling her a homewrecker, and other not-so-polite synonyms. Jason heard the commotion and came running to see what was going on. When he saw me cursing into the phone receiver, he snatched it from my hand.

"Hello?" he said, holding the phone up to his ear. "I'll call you back." He shut the phone and stared at me hard. I couldn't read the look on his face, and truthfully, I was too angry to even care how he felt.

"Oh, so now your girlfriend is just calling the house? Is that really what's happening here?" He smirked as if my fury was something amusing, a form of entertainment. That sent me over the edge. I picked up a can of cream of chicken soup and threw it, its contents splattering all over the counters and ripping a hole in the wall.

Jason didn't say a word. He just picked up his keys and walked out the door. The can of soup stayed lodged in the wall for weeks, neither one of us willing to clean up the mess we'd made. Every time I was in my kitchen, I had that stinky, soiled hole in the wall to remind me of the icy cavity in my chest that was growing colder with each passing day.

After that day, we both knew we'd reached a crossroads, a place where neither of us could even pretend we had a marriage left to save. The kids, who walked on tiptoe around us, unfortunately, had front row seats to our drama and dysfunction. As much as I wanted to shield them, I was lost in grief, hurt and pain so intense, I could only focus on breathing in and breathing out.

Finally, we decided to separate, to give each other space to determine what we wanted to do and how we wanted to move forward. It was a mild measure since we both stayed in the same house, he in the guest bedroom and I in the room we'd once shared. For the next few months, we stayed that way, living our separate lives under the same roof.

During that time, a dark cloud descended over everything for me. I felt like I had failed in life. God had given me everything I'd asked for, the family I'd spent years praying for, and I couldn't even keep that. I began to feel like maybe I wasn't meant to be happy. I wasn't meant to have this deeply cherished thing that other people had: somewhere to call home. What was it about me that seemed to drive people away? Why couldn't I ever just keep the thing I so desperately wanted?

My marriage was on the cusp of ruination. My kids would be forced to live two lives, in two homes – something I'd never wanted for them. An unceasing barrage of self-scathing thoughts ran through my mind. How would I make it in the world without him? How would I support myself, support my children? How would anyone else ever love me? Jason reminded me all the time: I was worthless, undesirable, used up. Maybe he was right. I would never get to possess happiness. 'That's the real problem,' I'd tell myself. 'You let yourself get greedy. You foolishly believed that you could have what everyone else has. Who do you think you are?'

I struggled to see a way out of my depression, this sadness that had permeated into every facet of my life. And one resounding thought ruled over my mind every day – I want to die. I began daydreaming about falling into a long, delicious sleep, one that I'd never wake up from. I saw myself clearly, fading away from the world as if I'd never even existed. Pretty soon, it was more than a fantasy. I began to plan my exit strategy. And one day, the answer came to me. I didn't need any complex ideas, all the tools were right at my fingertips.

A few days later, I went into my garage, which was connected to my house, and closed the door. Then I climbed into the driver's seat of my car, turned it on, reclined the seat and closed my eyes. I breathed deeply, taking in large, deliberate inhales. Silent tears flowed down my face. I kept my mind focused on one thought: sleep. I was so exhausted. Emotionally, physically, mentally. This was the right thing to do. It didn't make any sense to keep running like a mad woman towards people and things that seemed to only ever run away from me. My naive pursuit of happiness was coming to an irrevocable and definitive end. I began to tremble, my body coming to terms with what was happening. But I didn't move or get up. I tried to quiet my mind, to go back to a place of ease, to accept this fate that I was choosing. I could feel my body relaxing, getting heavier, and the weight of the pain of sacrifice lifting.

All of a sudden, Jason burst through the door from inside the house and pressed the automatic garage door opener. He reached inside my car and took out the keys, all the while covering his mouth with his shirt sleeve to avoid breathing in the toxic carbon monoxide that had been slowly filling the space. Then he carried me out of the car and into the house, slamming the door behind him.

By this point, I'd breathed in enough of the toxic fumes to feel the effects. I had a deep and persistent urge to vomit and I was so dizzy, that opening my eyes felt painful. Jason laid me down on the couch and opened all of the windows, instructing me to take deep breaths. I coughed uncontrollably, and it felt like my chest and throat were coated in something sticky and burning. I felt like I was choking.

After a few minutes had passed, the reality of what I had nearly succeeded at doing began to hit. And I sobbed uncontrollably, my children's faces flashing before my eyes. I was grateful that Jason had rescued me from that terrible fate, but I was also extremely upset that he'd driven me to that point in the first place. I'd been the best wife I could be to him, giving up my dreams and aspirations in pursuit of his. I doted on him and was supportive to a fault. And I'd forgiven him so many times, despite him repeatedly proving he wasn't worthy of it. When I tried to leave, he convinced me to stay. I took full responsibility for what I had almost done, the violence I had nearly unleashed on myself, but that didn't mean he was off the hook. He had mentally and emotionally abused me for years. And my resentment towards him grew even more intense.

After my attempt to die by suicide, I knew that I had to take control of my life, for the sake of my children. They needed me, and truthfully I needed them. They were my anchor, the one thing I could rely on to keep me tethered to the world regardless of anything going on around me. Jason seemed to have been shaken by the entire ordeal as well. We didn't talk about what had happened in detail, but he seemed to be more cautious around me, less dismissive of my feelings. It wasn't necessarily that he'd changed, just that he realized how much his actions were impacting me. I grew a little indifferent to our marriage, detaching myself so I could focus on my kids instead. I didn't have the strength to leave, terrified of how I'd ever support us all on my own.

By this point, we'd been living in Ringgold for about four years, and Jason had been working at his new job for just as long. But as it turned out, he didn't like civilian life as much as he thought he would. His job in finance required long hours in the office, where he was confined to his desk, staring at a computer screen. He missed the freedom he had with the military, the freedom to accept assignments and leave his family behind. The freedom to be a single man, when he felt like it. He told me that he wanted to return to the military. To say I was annoyed was an understatement. We'd uprooted our entire lives for him, yet again, so he could try something new, and here he was, changing his mind. But as usual, there wasn't much I could do but go along with his plans.

The only problem was that the closest military base was in Atlanta, two hours away from Ringgold. He suggested that the kids and I stay back so that they wouldn't have to leave school again, and he'd make the move on his own. I was tired of arguing with him, so reluctantly I agreed. The military found him an apartment and he got his life set up in Atlanta without us. On the weekends, we'd make the two-hour drive down to visit him, or he'd come to Ringgold to see us.

One weekend, the kids and I found ourselves in a precarious situation after locking ourselves out of the house in Ringgold. I called Jason a few times, trying to see if he knew where the spare key was, but he didn't answer. Reluctantly, I got into my car and started driving to Atlanta. It was not the ideal way to have a weekend together but I didn't have any other ideas as to what to do. When we finally arrived, it was around midnight. And once again, we found ourselves in a bit of a predicament. I didn't have keys to the apartment and Jason still wasn't there. We waited for over an hour, and at just past 1 am, he finally made his way home. It was immediately obvious to me that he'd been drinking, and I could tell from the sheepish look on his face that our presence outside his door was not only unexpected but unwanted as well.

Call it a woman's intuition, but I had the pressing feeling that he'd been out with another lady that night. I felt the feminine energy dripping from his entire body, the stench of betrayal wafting like cheap cologne from his skin. I gulped down my anger, determined to just get the kids inside and to sleep. Once they were settled, I questioned Jason, demanding to know where he'd been and who he'd been with. He denied being around any women that night, brushing off all of my concerns. But when I went into the bathroom, the evidence was everywhere. The cabinet was full of all of the things a woman would need to spend the night comfortably. Jason came up with some sorry excuse for why they were there. Despite how little work he put in to cover up his tracks, the man always had a convincing story ready and waiting. He was a master at story-telling, I'll give him that. Suffice it to say, I did not sleep in the same bed as him that night, preferring to lay down on the floor next to the kids. I knew another woman had been wrapped up in those sheets, her body intertwined with my husband's. The image was enough to make me sick to my stomach. Jason denied everything, but the clench in the pit of my belly was all of the proof I needed.

This merry-go-round of doubt, accusation, denial and pretending everything was normal went on for a few months. Eventually, I grew tired of being a single parent and of living in marriage limbo. What was the point of being married to someone I rarely ever saw, who my kids never got to spend any time with? DK, who was by now taller than his father, had just started his freshman year at Morehouse College. And Zii was about to enter high school, which was a big deal.

And I was certain that I didn't want her going through such a defining and important phase of her formative years in tiny old Ringgold. She deserved to be around people more like her, around folks she could actually relate to. Plus, I wanted to be closer to my family.

I also knew that Jason was still cheating on me, and our physical distance gave him ample freedom to do so without any fear. I wanted to nip any feelings of independence he was experiencing right in the bud. It wasn't much, but it felt like a tiny vindication, a minute form of retribution. I told Jason that I'd had enough and that he'd better find our family a house in Atlanta, we were moving there before Zii started high school. He could barely hide his disappointment, and I doubt that he even really tried. But he agreed.

I also told him that we were going to marriage counseling. The way we were living wasn't sustainable and our marriage was on the brink of collapse. It was clear to me we weren't capable of healing our relationship ourselves. I hoped that a neutral third party, a trained professional, could talk some sense into him because he sure as hell wasn't listening to me.

I found us a counselor and before we moved back to Atlanta we started having regular sessions once a week. I knew Jason was reluctant, so I intentionally picked a Black male counselor so that he'd feel more comfortable. Once a week, I'd drive to Atlanta for our sessions.

I'd expected that we'd go in, both share our truth, and he'd be able to tell him that what he was doing was wrong. I was open to the entire experience. I wanted to rehab our marriage. As Jason and I sat on the couch in his office, side by side, he settled into a couch across from us. As I lay bare the more than a decade of hurt he'd caused me, all of the cheating and betrayal I'd put up with, he watched me, a look of empathy on his face. When Jason's time to speak came, he somehow managed to turn the entire narrative on me, to gaslight and manipulate our therapist to the point where he was asking me if I was sure he'd actually done the things I was accusing him of. He assured the therapist that he was a doting husband and father, that he provided for us, and supported us in every way that he could. And the therapist ate up his lies with an eagerness that made me feel like I was losing my mind. We soon abandoned therapy as well.

Shortly after that, Zii, Jason and I moved into our new home in the south Atlanta suburb of Union City. The next few months were a strange departure from the norm. Jason wasn't going out much, other than to work. And he was so quiet, almost concerningly so. He became moody and would walk around the house, just sulking. He wasn't his usual self, but instead a moody, mopey version. It soon became apparent to me that Jason was depressed. I'd been in that position more times in my life than I could count, so it was easy for me to recognize.

I tried to talk to him, to ask him what was going on. I told him that I'd been depressed before too, and that I wanted to help him deal with whatever he was going through. But he wouldn't talk to me, at least not about anything of substance. One day, he told me that his mom was coming to visit, which was strange because she'd never visited us in any of our homes before. I prepared for her arrival as best as I could.

A few days after his mother had arrived, Jason got up and got ready dressed for work. Afterwards, he came over to my side of the bed and just sat there, next to me. The silence between us felt heavy and loaded. After a few minutes, he began to sob. I was bewildered. Tears streamed down his face and I stared at him, unsure what was going on. I tried to ask him what was wrong, but he just shook his head.

"Cathey," his voice shook as he spoke, "I've been cheating on you. I've been unfaithful. I'm so sorry." I blinked hard. I'd known for years that he was cheating, but he'd never actually come out and said it before. He'd never admitted it. And somehow his confession made his betrayal feel that much more acute, that more real and painful. He told me that he'd never meant to hurt me, that it was never his intention to cause me any suffering. He apologized, over and over again. He said they had met in the church parking lot and he had called it off. He no longer wanted to see her and his focus would be on me and his family.

I felt like throwing up. I'd wanted this day to come for years, for him to finally face up to what he'd done and to express real, genuine remorse. But now that it had happened, it didn't feel the way I'd hoped it would. I just felt empty, devoid of anything.

I asked him if it was over with her and he said yes. We agreed to talk more later and I told him that I wanted to be alone.

He nodded, got up and walked to the door, lingering there for a moment, then left. He drove Zii to the bus stop on the way, so I thought that I had the house to myself, that I'd have space to scream, cry, or do whatever I needed to do. But after finally conjuring the strength to drag myself out of bed, I heard moving around in the living room and remembered that my mother-in-law was staying with us. I sighed.

She called me into the living room and I could tell by the gentle tone in her voice that she knew. "Ah," I said to myself, "that's why she's here." He needed his mother to have his back. I shuffled over to where she was, and she gestured for me to sit next to her on the sofa. She turned towards me.

"Now, no marriage is perfect, and every marriage has its moments of infidelity," she said, pointing her finger toward me. "Cathey, are you really going to sit here and tell me you've never stepped out on Jason before?" I stared at her in disbelief. After what her son had just told me, her first response was to insist I'd probably cheated before too. It was just like her, to excuse the actions of her precious son.

"No, Mrs. Law, I haven't cheated on my husband, not ever," I spat back, standing up. "I have been faithful to him the entire time we've been together. I actually respect the sanctity of our vows." I charged out of the room, fuming. I was so angry, I felt like smoke was rising from my skin like I was one giant smoldering ember. "How dare she?", I huffed. I didn't know what to do, or how to deal with the firestorm of emotions building up inside me. How in the world was this woman going to look me in the face and try to normalize cheating? I knew I had to get out of that house, and far away from her.

I went to my room, packed a bag and waited for Jason to get home from work. When he arrived later that evening, I told him I was going away for a few days. I could see the shock on his face, his eyes searching mine for answers, for some clue as to where my head was at. But I kept a straight face as I picked up my bag, brushing past him to the front door. I got into my car and started the long drive towards Helen, Georgia. I had booked myself a hotel in the mountains, somewhere I could clear my head. I spent the next few days just breathing in the crisp, fresh air, walking through the lush forests and soaking in the spa bathtub in the center of my hotel bedroom.

I thought about the future, about what I would do. Years before, I'd spoken with one of our ministers about divorce and what the Bible had to say about it. He told me that there were two legitimate grounds for divorce: adultery and abandonment of God. He'd asked me if my marriage fell within either of these two categories. I couldn't meet his eyes, but I nodded my head yes. I hadn't been able to face it before, but now I knew that Jason had no more cards to play. I decided then that because Jason had finally confessed, something he'd failed to do for years, I was willing to move forward with our marriage. To me, a confession and repentance signaled a readiness to change. It meant that he actually felt guilty and was taking action to remedy the situation. This was more than he'd ever done before. But if he was unfaithful to me *one more time*, I'd leave. No questions asked.

After a few days, I headed back home to Atlanta. As soon as I stepped foot in the house, Jason began. He told me that he was sorry, again, and I held my hand up to silence him.

"Just stop. Please. I don't need to hear how sorry you are Jason. I've heard it enough times. I just need you to show me that you mean it." He nodded, putting his head down in shame. He promised me that he was a changed man, and that soon enough, I'd realize it too.

Over the next few months, Jason put in a real effort to improve our relationship. We began going on dates, to talk more, and learn about each other again. Things seemed to be on the mend. Despite the multitude of highs and lows we experienced, he seemed genuinely dedicated to staying married, a fact that contributed to my resolution to stay. When things were good between us, they were really good. I lived for those times, for the moments of love and affection we shared. And when things were bad again, which they always inevitably were, I'd cling to my memories, holding onto them with a desperation that bordered on insanity. I was convinced that if we could just return to that happiness once more, eventually it would become permanent. He'd realize how marvelous we could be together, and he'd stay with me.

Three years after moving to Atlanta, I finally felt like I'd settled into a decently content routine. DK was finishing up his final semester in college and Zii was about to enter her senior year of high school. I was working at a job that I loved. We moved into another home closer to the heart of Atlanta and Zii's high school. And importantly, things between Jason and I had been going very, very well. We'd been on an upward swing for over a year, and I was confident that this time, he'd truly changed. For once, I wasn't holding my breath, waiting for the ball to drop. I thought that I'd finally gotten my husband back.

One day, as I was in our room making the bed, Jason walked in, his mouth drawn into a frown and his eyebrows lifted sheepishly. I recognized it, the look on his face. He was about to tell me something I didn't want to hear. I braced myself for the worst.

"Cathey, I'm being deployed to Iraq," he said. "I can't get promoted to the next rank if I can't show wartime service." I let out a small gasp. It wasn't what I'd been expecting. It was worse. He pulled me in close and hugged me, told me that everything would be fine. I didn't know what to say, or how to respond. I knew that it was true, he would have to serve to get promoted. And he had been feeling quite stationary lately like his career had come to a standstill. So I understood where he was coming from. And yet, I was still angry.

"Why now, when things are going so well between us?" I asked, desperation dripping from my tongue. "Zii is a senior in high school, she needs her dad. *I need you.*" He stared at me with a gentle glint in his eyes. He told me he understood, but it was only temporary. He needed this to get promoted. And he assured me that he'd be back mid-year, just in time for Zii's graduation. There was nothing I could do, his mind was already made up. So I nodded dutifully.

Over the next few weeks, we had several conversations about how we'd stay in contact while he was gone. He reiterated over and over again that he'd likely be out of commission once in a while, that sometimes the barracks would be on lockdown, and all forms of communication turned off. War was a messy thing, and they had procedures in place to limit the flow (or leak) of information. I tried to wrap my head around everything. This was our new reality, and I didn't have time to linger on the details.

For the first few months, things went by as smoothly as they could, given the circumstances. DK had graduated from Morehouse and was now back at home while he interned at a local law firm. The three of us, DK, Zii and I adjusted to Jason's absence. Luckily, we'd had years of practice.

But this time, unlike every other time, Jason was in a real warzone. He was in active combat and danger wasn't just a real risk and possibility, it was a likelihood. Jason was at war. *Jason could die.* These were the thoughts that stayed, like a shadow, in the back of my mind at almost all times. When a few days passed by and he didn't call us on Skype, my worries became a looming dark cloud that hung over my every waking moment.

One day, after there had been a lull in communication for more than three days, I became deeply concerned. Had something happened to him, I wondered. I considered all of the worst-case scenarios. I envisioned my doorbell ringing, and three uniformed officers standing on the other side, holding their hats over their hearts as they revealed the terrible news. In some of my imaginings, the kids answered the door and the sound of their screams, though only in my mind, would make me cry. This is when I decided to check his email, to see if he had been online. And that's when I discovered that he was fine. More than fine, actually. He was *still* cheating on me.

As I was grappling with fears that he was dead, he was sending webcams to Beverly. Immediately, I knew that the marriage was over. My *one more time* had come, and instinctively, I knew I was done. After years of forgiving and forgetting, of shifting my threshold to withstand just a little bit more pain, more betrayal, more torment, I'd finally reached my breaking point. There was no turning back this time. No more working on our relationship, no more hope, no more healing, no amount of prayer could save us. Our marriage was broken beyond repair.

I had no idea how I would navigate life alone, how I'd be a single mom, a self-supporting woman. But I also knew that I had no choice. Staying wasn't an option anymore. For years, our relationship had been chipping away at my sense of self. I did not know who Cathey was anymore, and if I didn't make a move my indecision would kill me.

The next time he called me, a few days later, I unleashed. I told him I knew about everything: Beverly, the webcam, the continued infidelity. At first, he denied everything and insisted it wasn't true, that there must have been some kind of misunderstanding. But I wasn't hearing it. This time, his manipulation wouldn't work on me. I told him that it was over. I wanted a divorce. He was silent on the other end of the line for a minute before hanging up. He didn't call again, didn't try to fix things or to convince me to give it another shot. He must have heard the finality in my voice, the sureness of my decision.

He immediately went into self-protection mode. Within a few weeks, he shut off all financial support and all sources of communication. He made significantly more money than I did, and we'd divided our earnings in such a way that his paycheque would go towards paying for the house, and mine to utilities, bills and any other additional expenses. But all of a sudden, I had no access to the money I needed to pay for our home and no way to contact him. I couldn't afford to pay for our home with my income alone, so I knew eventually, we'd have to move to something within my range.

He also rushed to file for divorce before I did, as if to prove a point, or to indicate that he was somehow the one who'd made this decision. When I opened my door one day to find a sheriff standing there, serving me divorce papers, I felt a sting of hurt, followed by rage.

Somehow, his cold-blooded response only solidified my resolve and made me even more sure that I'd made the right decision. It was like all of a sudden, the mask was off and I saw him for who he really was. I had the creeping realization that I was seeing him for the first time, that the man I'd been desperately clinging to for all of those years was nothing more than an illusion. I couldn't fathom someone I once loved so deeply being so vindictive, so cutthroat that they'd even cut off support to their children. It wasn't even only the money. He never made any effort to have a conversation with me at any point, to try and navigate our divorce maturely. As the kids say, he just ghosted me.

This all happened, inconveniently, right before Zii's high school graduation. Jason returned to the U.S. a few months later, and he never came home, not even to say hello to his kids, a fact that crushed me, as well as them. He went straight to Beverly's home. I knew this because I drove over to where she lived on a hunch. Sure enough, I saw his friend's car in the driveway. The front door to the house was wide open and I could see inside. I saw them sitting there on the sofa, and I even heard Jason's voice, a voice that suddenly sounded like it was laced with knives.

On the afternoon of Zii's graduation, I did not expect that he'd show up at all. As I walked through the crowd at the end of the ceremony, intent on taking some photos with my kids to commemorate the day, Zii and DK walked towards me looking solemn. I asked DK what had happened and he'd told me that they'd seen their dad after all. Zii had rushed towards him, crying, both excited and shocked to see him. The only words she could manage between her tears were "Daddy, why?", a question he was never able to answer. As I later heard from other parents, he did not look well and reeked of alcohol. I surmised that his guilt had been overwhelming. So much so that he couldn't face his children without a bit of liquid courage.

Meanwhile, I was dealing with my debilitating existential dread. The first few months after we separated passed in a teary, rage-filled haze. Now that I'd finally decided to leave my toxic marriage, I was forced to face the truth about the woman I'd become. There were times when I looked in the mirror and barely recognized the face staring back at me. It's a sobering experience to see a stranger in your reflection. It broke my heart to finally confront all of the ways I'd betrayed my soul, especially for a man who did not deserve it.

For a while, it was hard to even get out of bed, depression setting into my bones like a cancer. As soon as I got home from work, I'd strip off my clothes, throw them into a pile on the floor and bury myself under the covers to weep. Quickly, the house, as if in sync with my emotional state, fell into a state of disarray.

I felt that I had let my life slip out of my grasp, that it was something I was no longer in control of. I wished I'd done more to prepare, to protect myself. But I believed so strongly, so hopelessly, in the permanence of our marriage. I truly never thought it would come to this. And now that it had, I didn't know what to do. I didn't know how to move through the world as a single woman, especially not at 46 years old. I had no clue of what it would take to be a single mother. In fact, for that first little while, I could barely muster up the energy to be a parent at all.

When I told my kids that we were getting divorced, they were numb. Even though I tried to shield them from our dysfunction, kids are smart. They're intuitive, and they know far more than we give them credit for. I think they were more shocked that I'd finally made a decisive decision, that after 20 years of arguments and verbal altercations, I finally stood up for myself.

Still, even though they weren't surprised, our divorce devastated them, in the way that a loved one is devastated to find out someone they cherished finally succumbed to a terminal illness. They knew it was coming, but it still broke them when it happened. They were losing something irreplaceable: their family unit. And it breaks my heart to say that, at least in the beginning, it was them who took care of me.

As I lay locked up in my room, the mess piling up around me, my kids tiptoed throughout the house, doing their best not to disturb me in my era of mourning. They knew I needed a bit of space and time to process the big feelings that came with a divorce. And my children, the joys and lights of my life, are what helped me get through to the other side. I apologized to them profusely, begging them to forgive me for not being stronger. And they showered me with love, insisting I had nothing to be sorry for. They knew I was doing my best, given the circumstances.

After a few months, I knew I had to make a change, to channel my immense sadness into something other than tears. I turned to the treadmill, collecting dust in the garage, for solace. And every day, instead of climbing into bed, I'd lace up my sneakers, put in my headphones, and walk. Hours would pass, day turning into night, with me out there, making my slow trek back towards myself. With every long stride, I pondered the future, allowing myself the space to contemplate my fears, to reflect on where I was and where I wanted to be.

And truthfully, I was terrified. I was 46 years old. Wasn't I too old to begin again? I wasn't a young woman anymore. How would I go at it alone? For years before I finally mustered up the courage to leave, Jason, sensing that my patience with him was wearing thin, would say things to me to destroy my confidence. "Who's going to want you if you leave? At your age, and with two young kids?", he'd snicker. After I left, those words came back to me with a vengeance, taunting me into periods of paralyzing self-doubt. What if he was right? What if I couldn't do it or if I wasn't up to the task?

Fortunately, all of those fears and uncertainties paled in comparison to the terror I felt at continuing on that same trajectory, of remaining in that spiral of dysfunction and disrespect. I realized, in those long hours walking on my treadmill, that being alone wasn't so bad when the alternative was a cheating partner and a devastatingly unhappy marriage. If there's one thing Jason taught me, it's that you don't have to be alone to feel lonely.

I felt myself becoming stronger, both physically and emotionally. As I began working through the depths of my pain, I realized that there was so much more, layers and layers of trauma that had compounded over the years into a dense brick of emotional damage. I knew that it would take time to fully heal, but for one of the first times in my life, I was at least willing to face it all.

Slowly but surely, I gained a sense of normalcy. I was rediscovering myself and it was a brilliant, beautiful process. At the same time, I still had my divorce to deal with, and my grief to address. But just when I thought things were looking up, I suffered another immense loss.

My aunt Marguerite, the matriarch of our family, died. Her passing broke me in a way I didn't expect. She was a pillar of strength in all of our lives, and knowing she was gone forever knocked me off keel. Anytime I was back home in Mobile, her home (and her presence) was always the first place I wanted to return to. She'd been sick for a few years, and my sisters and nephew had been taking care of her. By the end, she wasn't able to speak very much, but we still enjoyed each other's company any time I was able to make it back home to visit. All of my memories of her came back to me in a flood of flashbacks. Her creativity and her faith, her enduring love of baseball, her warmth. Aunt Marguerite was the third mother I lost in my life and adjusting to the reality I'd never be able to return to her tender embrace was hard to swallow.

Jason, though he'd known Aunt Marguerite for more than 20 years and had even spent many days and nights in her home, didn't acknowledge her passing at all. He didn't send a card or flowers – not even a phone call. I hadn't expected much from him, and yet he still found a way to disappoint me.

The only thing I could do at that time was to lean heavily on my children. Despite all of the sadness we'd all experienced, or perhaps because of it, we grew closer than ever. DK had moved back in with me shortly before the divorce as he worked at an internship in the city, while Zii was studying at Howard University in D.C. My kids were my anchors, reminding me constantly of how strong I was, and pushing me to give myself more credit. They challenged me to love myself, to delve deeper into the depths of who I was, and to pursue what I loved with reckless abandon. Our relationships blossomed as we all, together, began to understand ourselves better.

Later that year, in the fall of 2010, I was trying to figure out how I could help Zii come home for Thanksgiving. I'd budgeted enough money to get her home for Christmas, but with my meager income and the pile of bills building up, I didn't think I could afford to bring her home for the November holiday as well. At first, we'd agreed that she would just spend Thanksgiving in D.C. with some friends. But at the last minute, she called to let me know that her hallmate's family would be driving to Alabama for the Thanksgiving weekend and they'd offered to drop her off in Atlanta. I was elated – I'd never spent a Thanksgiving away from Zii before, and now this meant both my kids would be home.

A few days later, she arrived. I headed outside to meet her hallmates and their family and to thank them for giving Zii a ride. The two girls stood on the curb with their Dad, a man we'll call Ayomide, who'd been driving. Being from the South, I'm a big hugger, so I reached out and gave him a tight hug, expressing my gratitude for bringing my baby to me. I noticed that he'd paused during the hug, had pulled me in a bit closer and lingered for a second. I didn't think much of it.

Not long after, Zii sat with me in the kitchen, staring at her phone as I cut up some vegetables. She giggled, and looked up towards me, a smirk on her face and a mischievous glint in her eyes. I lifted my eyebrow and asked what was up.

"Someone has a crush on you," she shrieked, sidling up next to me.

"What? Who?" I asked, wiping my hands on my apron.

"Ayomide! He's been talking about you to the girls non-stop. They said he wants your phone number. Can I give it to him?" Zii looked up at me, a hopeful smile on her face.

"Absolutely not!" I shouted, laughing. I was flattered, and a little intrigued, but I wasn't quite ready to let another man into my life just yet. When he and his girls pulled up to pick up Zii and take her back to D.C. with them, things between us were a little awkward. I knew he had a crush on me, and I didn't want to lead him on so I dialed back my southern hospitality. But over the next month, Ayomide persisted, asking for my phone number incessantly. Eventually, I relented and let him have it. Why not, I finally told myself. You deserve a little fun. He called me soon after, and we began talking daily. A few weeks later, he drove down to Atlanta from D.C. and took me out on a date.

He was the perfect gentleman, opening doors for me and pulling out my chair. The restaurant he picked, Two Urban Licks, was sophisticated and sexy, with dim lights and tiny tables that were cramped together. We sat facing each other, a golden glow illuminating everything. It felt easy and organic to talk to him. There were no awkward lulls in the conversation, no pauses where we both stared at our phones because we didn't know what to say. The conversation flowed easily and we spent the entire night captivated by each other, laughing and conversing about everything. At the end of the night, when we were standing at the valet waiting for his car, he wrapped his arms around me from behind, enveloping me in a warm embrace. It was strange but I felt so comfortable and so safe with him, like I'd known him for years.

The next day, he took me go-carting and made fun of my driving skills. We spent the whole afternoon in a fit of giggles. The entire time we were together, I don't think I stopped smiling once. Early that evening, he got in his car and got ready to drive back to D.C. As he pulled out of the driveway, I stood outside waving goodbye. He stopped his car in the middle of the street, hopped out and ran towards me.

"I just needed to get one more hug," he smiled, taking me into his arms and pulling me close. It was one of the cutest moments I'd ever experienced. I felt giddy, like a young girl who had a crush on a boy. We fell for each other fast and hard. After that, we began a long-distance relationship. Sometimes I'd fly to D.C. to see him, and other times he'd come to Atlanta.

I felt like I'd entered a new season of my life, one I never, ever thought I'd experience. I was in a healthy and happy relationship. I soon found out that as terrified as I'd been of independence, I was quite good at it. And I enjoyed it. I wasn't fully comfortable with my financial situation just yet, as I was still living in the house Jason and I had shared. And it was more money than I could afford to pay. But for the first time in my life, I trusted God so fully and completely, I wasn't afraid of what was going to happen. Somehow, intuitively, I just knew things would work themselves out. And oddly enough, they did.

A few months after the split, my job reached out to me and asked if I'd be interested in relocating to Orlando, Florida, all expenses paid, to lead HR for their office out there. Of course, I said yes. A fresh start in a new city was exactly what I needed. And now, I'd be free of the burden of paying for the house, and away from all of the ugly energy I'd felt being in Atlanta.

Ayomide came down from D.C. and helped DK and I pack up the house and all of our things. And together we made the drive to Orlando. I loved living in Florida. I loved being able to go to the beach on the weekends, to sit by the water and just meditate, and breathe in the salty air. Things in my life were falling into place, aligning in a way that gave me so much confidence.

However, as happy as I was with my new life, I couldn't lean into it completely – at least not yet. I still had one thing shackling me to my old life: Jason and I weren't divorced yet. We'd been going through mediation, trying to agree on what I was entitled to. But Jason was extremely hostile, not wanting to budge, unwilling to let me get a cent. Unfortunately for him, that wasn't in his control.

Before leaving for Orlando, I had done some research and found a lawyer who claimed to be experienced with military law to help me with my case. A military divorce is a little more nuanced than a regular divorce, and it was important that I found someone who understood those laws thoroughly. It became clear, after several failed attempts at mediation, where I had to drive the five hours back to Atlanta from Florida, that we'd have to take our case to court. We weren't going to come to any kind of agreement, so we'd leave it to a judge to decide.

On the day of our trial, I was nervous and could barely keep my hands from trembling. I'd never been in a courtroom before and the whole experience seemed so daunting, so intimidating. As I sat next to my lawyer on one side of the courtroom, Jason, his lawyer and his sister sat on the other. Jason was trying to prevent me from getting a portion of his retirement pension, something I was entitled to as his wife for 24 years and for the entire duration of his time in service. His lawyer called me to the stand, and attempted to grill me on my career. She asked me what I had studied, where I had worked, and what my career prospects looked like. It was clear to me that she was trying to establish that I had the means to support myself, and didn't need Jason's money.

I looked at his lawyer, at the smug and self-satisfied look on her face. And I looked at Jason, staring at me with a look of contempt.

"I don't have a career," I began, looking up at the judge as I spoke. "You see, for the past 24 years of my life, I have followed this man wherever he wanted to go. I've moved with him across the country, across the world even, from state to state, station to station. I had to sacrifice my career aspirations to keep our family together, so we could all follow the whims and impulses of my husband. I have never been able to establish tenure at any company, because our constant moving around prevented me from being anywhere long enough to do that." After Jason had completed his MBA, following our move to Ringgold, it was supposed to be my turn to focus on my career, my turn to be the priority. But he was always busy being busy, and he refused to take responsibility for the kids in the way he'd promised so that plan never came to fruition. I told all of this to the judge, reliving my neglect as if it was brand new, a fresh wound.

The judge nodded, and his lawyer looked annoyed, as though she hadn't been expecting that of me. By this point in my life, I knew that I had to advocate for myself and that I couldn't trust anyone else to do that for me. And in the end, it worked.

The judge ruled that I was entitled to a sizable portion of his pension, spousal support for a year and that I'd get to keep my military ID. That meant I could still access certain military programs and services, including healthcare.

When the judge announced his decision, Jason quickly got up and stormed out of the courtroom. After more than 20 years of marriage, that was how things finally ended between us, with Jason huffing off in a fit of rage and frustration.

I felt like I'd finally gotten the justice I deserved. Jason had wanted a wife who would sit idly by as he went off and did whatever he wanted. And as soon as I'd decided I didn't want to be that woman for him anymore, he thought he could just throw me out like yesterday's trash. I felt vindicated, like the entire universe had conspired in my favor to show him what I was really worth. And he'd spend the rest of his life paying the price.

But perhaps more importantly, I felt that I'd officially closed the door on that chapter of my life, that I could walk away knowing I'd fought like hell. For the first time in my life, *I felt alive – and free.*

CHAPTER 6

Climbing the Ladder to Nowhere

There is something about salty air and the sound of ocean waves crashing on the beach that heals me. When I was a little girl, grappling with debilitating grief and guilt, I'd sit on the sandy shoreline and dream of the future. When I was so hurt by my life that I went mute, the sea provided a respite, a place where the silence felt like freedom.

After getting divorced when I was 46, I returned to the sea often. The silence that was a balm to my soul as a child, returned to me in the ebbs and flows of the foamy water. It was there, with my toes in the sand, that I began to make peace with my past. I let go of the shame and guilt from my mother's death, and the feelings of worthlessness stemming from my marriage. I gained incredible clarity about myself and what I wanted from my life. I realized while sitting there one morning that I had to end things with Ayomide.

He'd been a breath of fresh air in my life at a time when I felt suffocated by fear. At one point, for a short season in my life, he showed me real, genuine and healthy love. He opened my eyes to what it meant and felt like to be desired, appreciated and cared for by a man. Unfortunately, our relationship wasn't one destined to last forever. As great as he'd been to me, I eventually began to feel like he wasn't able to offer me the things that I needed. After dating for a year, I knew our season was over and we broke up.

Despite being single again, I was enjoying the process of rediscovering myself and identifying what made me happy. Living in Orlando gave me the space to understand what I needed to feel fulfilled. It's also where I realized that if I wanted to do more than scratch the surface, I needed to reach out for help. I needed to talk to someone. My only experience with therapy at this point had been the couple's therapist Jason and I saw, which was awful. He'd gaslit me and dismissed my very real suffering in the same way Jason had, insisting that perhaps my marriage wasn't as bad as I'd been making it out to be. But still, I tried not to let that lousy incident color this new attempt at healing.

Therapy was a challenge for me at first. I was so uncomfortable with the act of opening up, of sharing my emotions with a stranger, with someone I didn't know if I could trust. I chose a Black woman as my therapist because I felt like she'd understand me better than a therapist of any other race. And after meeting with her for our first appointment, I already felt a shift. For the first time in a long time, I felt seen, heard and understood. And the more we spoke, the more I began to uncover invisible core beliefs I held about myself, ideas that defined how I acted and reacted throughout my life. Together, we worked through my deep, persistent feelings of guilt and shame. Unbeknownst to me, I'd carried them with me since I was a little girl. I'd never thought about how guilt over my mother's death had shaped me, how my shame had made me believe I was unworthy, and had allowed me to accept crumbs of affection rather than real love. But she helped me see that I wasn't responsible for what had happened to my mom. I had no control over how I was born, and neither did my mother. It was just how life happened sometimes.

My therapist taught me techniques to let go of my shame and guilt, these traits that did nothing to serve me. She taught me how to meditate, to quiet the barrage of anxious thoughts that moved through my mind incessantly. I'd practice role-playing, having conversations with my mom, with Jason, where I got to share my deepest fears, the things I felt, and to respond to myself in a way that helped me obtain closure. It wasn't a quick process. I was working through a lifetime of hurt, after all. But I gained the tools to deal with my emotions, instead of being buried by them.

Therapy also helped me to grow even closer to my children, who were also learning more about what they wanted from their lives. We were all gaining insight into ourselves, and leaning on each other for support. I was in constant awe of how brave they both were (and still are) and how courageously they went after their dreams. They were so introspective about their futures, and they weren't afraid to forge their own paths and live in a way that aligned with their purpose, no matter how unconventional. They had a natural and wide-eyed curiosity about the world and themselves that inspired me and made me proud to call them mine.

But this isn't to say that their self-discoveries didn't challenge me as well. When Zii was in college, she decided to do a semester abroad in South Africa. I was supportive of that decision, as I knew the value of traveling. Obviously, I had my fears, but I knew I'd raised her well enough to hold her own. One day, when I was sitting in my office at work, she called me and we chatted for a few minutes. After discussing how our lives were going, she fell silent on the other end.

"Mommy," she said, her voice low and nervous, "I have something to tell you." I sat back in my chair, bracing myself.

"I'm queer and I'm non-binary," she said, quickly. It was clear it was something she'd been wanting to get off of her chest for some time. I blinked, not quite understanding.

"What does that mean?" I asked, clutching my phone even closer. She went on to explain that she didn't identify as a woman or a man, that her identity was more fluid, a spectrum and not a solid, concrete thing. She told me that she was dating a woman. I listened, but my brain struggled to grasp all of the things she was saying. I had never heard so many of these terms before. It was as if she was speaking to me in a different language. I told her that we'd talk more about it later, when I wasn't at work and had more time to delve into the details. We hung up and I quickly got up and closed my office door, sat back at my desk, and sobbed. I didn't know what to think.

So, she's gay, I told myself. But what did it mean to be non-binary? I didn't understand what it meant for her to not identify as a woman. Truthfully, it took me a while to fully comprehend that just because I gave birth to a little girl, that wasn't what *they* were, it wasn't an identity they identified with.

We spoke more and they explained that they didn't go by *she/her* pronouns anymore. It was *they*. I tried to be understanding, to ask the questions that were spiraling in my mind in the gentlest way I could. But I was confused. I didn't understand their vocabulary or the language they used to describe themselves.

My feelings for my child didn't change in the least bit with this revelation. They were still my baby, and my heart still ached with tenderness for them. But that didn't stop me from wondering if I had done something wrong. Was it because of the divorce? Had Jason and I breaking up caused them to question their identity, to reach for answers to their sadness outside of our family?

It took me some time to grasp that it had nothing to do with me, with us, that no one was 'at fault', as I first believed. Zii was simply listening to the call of their soul, aligning themselves with an identity that felt more accurate. It took months of learning, and unlearning, and relearning, to gain a comfortable understanding of Zii. And it's something I worked at, and still work on, every day. I make mistakes often, using the wrong pronouns, calling them by a name they no longer associate with. It hasn't been easy, but I do my best.

My relationship with Zii struggled for a little while, as I grappled with my misconceptions. But my children are the most important things in my life. And we've since managed to deepen and strengthen our bond, gaining newfound respect and admiration for each other. I'm constantly in awe of Zii, of their courage to be who they are without apology; fully, freely and intensely.

After moving with me to Orlando, DK realized that law school no longer fit the path he wanted to go down. He wanted to explore, to do something that gave him more freedom to travel. He came across an opportunity to move to China to teach English and applied. Until that was approved, he got a job at UPS on the evening shift. A few months later, his visa for China was approved and he had his ticket to fly to Shanghai. Zii, for their part, was finishing up college in D.C. and preparing to move to New York afterwards.

For the first time in my life, I was completely on my own. At first, it was a strange transition, adjusting to the silence of living alone. It wasn't how I imagined I'd be spending my life as an empty nester. For one, I always thought that Jason and I would be enjoying this time together. I thought we'd travel more, and lean into the freedom of just being a couple for the first time in our lives while watching our kids grow into their own people.

But soon, I grew to enjoy doing it solo. I finally started my graduate degree, taking classes at night. I was spending my days working at a job I loved, going for walks near the beach and strengthening my faith. I'd talk to God all of the time, confiding my deepest fears, laying my soul bare. And often, I'd hear His faint whispers back, quiet murmurs that He had so much more in store for me. But early one Saturday morning, it wasn't a whisper that spoke to me but a loud and clear voice that woke me up from my sleep. I shot straight up in my bed and heard a booming voice say, 'I have so much more for you. I'm going to reveal things to you that will blow your mind. But it's not here. It's not here.' I began to tremble, terrified of what I'd just experienced. I asked God 'If not here, then where?' but no response came – at least not then. I kept listening, waiting for the answer. One day, it came, but not in the way I expected.

My company at the time had been downsizing, and somehow I managed to survive a few rounds of layoffs. But I felt it in my core that my luck was running out. At the same time, a friend and colleague told me she was transferring to Dallas, Texas since the market there was so much better. And she suggested I consider doing the same. I'd never even thought about moving to Texas before, but I figured it was worth a shot. I'd just completed my graduate degree and felt the move might really benefit me. I approached my manager and asked if a transfer to Dallas was possible. Much to my surprise, they agreed.

So in 2015, after 4 years of living in Orlando, I packed up my things and made my next big move. I rented a ranch-style house in Frisco, a newer suburb of Dallas. My neighborhood was lovely and quiet, full of retirees and families. A similar feeling grew within me, this was good for a season but a fire still ran through my blood for something more.

Shortly after moving there, Zii graduated from college and came to live with me for a few months before moving to New York. Initially, they were intent on becoming an attorney. But near the end of their degree, they'd realized they wanted to pursue a more creative endeavor, specifically dance. Since they could walk, they'd been enrolled in dance classes and it was an enduring, life-long passion. They realized that traditional employment in corporate America didn't align with what they wanted for their life and decided to commit themselves fully to being a creative. At first, I was reluctant to get on board. How would they support themselves? How would they make enough money to stand on their own two feet? But I could see Zii's resolve, how committed they were to following their heart, to not falling victim to a life of convenience rather than purpose. And I quickly changed my tune, encouraging them to do what would make them happy.

At the same time, my problems with corporate America were just beginning. Five months into my move to Dallas, I got laid off from my job. Part of the reason I'd transferred to Texas was because I felt I'd be safeguarded from the fate that inevitably found me anyway. You can't outrun or outsmart your destiny, I'd chuckled to myself after receiving the bad news. What made things even worse was that I'd been with my company for nearly seven years, and I really loved my job. Despite the way things ended, the company had been hyper-supportive during my entire tenure with them. They'd always encouraged my advancement, had pushed me to believe in myself more and in the talent I possessed. Truthfully, I thought that I'd stay with the company for many more years, potentially until retirement.

Getting laid off was a really big blow. I had finally settled comfortably into the routine of supporting myself, of being an independent woman. And I reveled in it. I loved the fact that I didn't depend on anyone but myself. But now, I was unemployed and I had to figure something out, and fast. I'd received a severance package when my company let me go, which was a nice cushion while I tried to determine where to go next. There was a part of me that was terrified. I was already starting over in a new city, and now I had to find a new job too. But the more I thought about it, the more confident I became.

I'd persevered through far more challenging situations than this. Plus, I was educated, had a master's degree, and a ton of experience. Any company would have been lucky to have me. Within a few months of my job search, I landed a great role at a company as the Regional HR Director. I enjoyed my job. And now that I was employed again, I began to enjoy living in Dallas as well.

After living in the suburbs for one year, I realized I wanted to be more centrally located, to have a more walkable lifestyle closer to the action. When the lease for my house was up in 2016, I found an apartment in uptown on Lemmon Avenue, a main thoroughfare in Dallas. It was a big shift from living in the suburbs. In my Lemmon Avenue apartment, as soon as

I stepped outside my building's front door, I was in the belly of the entertainment district. Restaurants, bars, movie theaters and clothing shops lined the streets. If I wanted to have a night out, my options were unlimited. And the best part was I could be back home in no time without ever needing to get into my car. I loved living there, especially as a single woman. But after a while, I began to crave the quiet of the suburbs, of having my own space. My apartment began to feel like a fishbowl, and my neighbors, many of whom were young adults attracted to the thrills of the party lifestyle, were incessantly encroaching on my peace.

After a year of living in Uptown, I felt ready to make a big life move. I was tired of renting houses, signing a lease every year, packing up my stuff and moving from home to home. I had a good job, with a steady, comfortable income. In 2017, I bought my first house. It was a huge accomplishment for me. Just a few years prior, I was grappling with how in the world I'd be able to survive on my own after depending on my husband for nearly two decades. Now, I was completely self-reliant and making one of life's biggest and most important purchases alone. It was one of the best feelings I'd ever experienced in my entire life. For so many years of my life, I'd doubted myself and my abilities. I'd gone from feeling worthless, co-dependent and plagued with guilt, to being completely free, confident and self-sufficient. There were days I woke up and felt like I was living in a dream, one I'd had as a little girl. I'd pinch myself just so I could be reminded that I'd built this life for myself. I was the author of this fairytale I was currently living. I was the hero of my own story.

The house was far larger than anything a single woman needed, but I loved it. It was a two-level, four bedroom, three and a half bath home. It had an office and a beautiful kitchen where I spent all of my time. My kids both had their own rooms for when they returned to visit and if any of my sisters came to stay, they'd have their choice of bedroom as well. I had a large backyard where I eventually installed some raised beds and planted an assortment of vegetables and flowers in the front and back yard. Whenever I needed to feel grounded, I'd go back there and sink my hands into the dirt. I loved the process of fertilizing the soil, planting a seed, nourishing its environment and patiently waiting for life to flourish.

When I wasn't pinching myself for how far I'd come, or spending time in my garden, I dedicated a lot of my free time to decorating my home and traveling with my two oldest sisters, April and Anitra. If any of us had a work trip we had to go on, the other two would tag along and make a vacation out of it. We went to Chicago, D.C., Houston and Myrtle Beach. Since they are also my sorority sisters, we'd often attend Boule together. It was a deeply enriching time in my life.

Despite everything else I had going on, my real focus was my career. I had aspirations of advancing my way through the ranks and one day becoming Chief HR Officer for the whole company. I wanted to work my way to the top. By this point in my life, I'd stopped installing ceilings on my goals; I knew that I was capable of anything I set my mind to. The only problem was that my workplace wasn't the most supportive or inclusive environment. I knew that if I wanted to move up, to get the position I really wanted, I had to go somewhere else. I found a new job, somewhere I thought I'd be appreciated, where I could move through the ranks. Things didn't turn out the way I'd expected though.

When I was first interviewing for my job, I spoke with the COO of the company on the phone and he asked me what school I'd obtained my master's degree from. After I was hired, and we met face to face, he asked me the question about my education again. It threw me because I could feel the racial overtones, the way he inspected me as he asked. After I told him, he smirked, ever so slightly. "I guess that's a good school," he shrugged, dismissively. I felt a sting of embarrassment, which I quickly gulped down. His comment was even more upsetting when I realized that my boss was a White woman who'd never even gone to college. I looked around me, taking stock of the demographic makeup of the company, especially within leadership roles. The lack of diversity was blatant and impossible to miss. But I wasn't one to see a problem and simply gawk at it. I knew that there was a way to remedy the situation, to create a more inclusive and equitable workplace.

I approached one of my superiors at the company about spearheading a Diversity, Equity and Inclusion (DE&I) initiative at the company, but was promptly rebuffed. I was annoyed, considering I had both the passion and the talent to help my company address the glaring racial disparities within their ranks. Their lack of interest disturbed me, but I brushed it off and went back to focusing all of my energy on advancing within my role. But even that was more difficult than I felt it should have been. I was one of the only Black women in the office at my level. There was plenty of diversity among the hourly staff, but we were few and far between the higher the salary got. I was either being tokenized for my race or forced to work twice as hard as everyone else to achieve the same rewards and promotions.

I was well aware that my sentiments weren't unique to me either. Dozens of studies have been done on the struggles and challenges Black women face in corporate America. The findings are a sobering reminder of just how alive and rampant racial injustice and inequality are. According to research from Lean In, an organization dedicated to closing the gender pay gap and creating more equitable workplaces, 21% of women C-suite leaders today are women. And only 1% of those are Black.[3] We have fewer mentoring opportunities and are less likely to have supportive relationships with managers and supervisors.

Black women face microaggressions almost daily, from comments about our hair and makeup to how we dress and our manner of speech. And because of the ever-persistent racist trope of the 'angry Black woman,' speaking out becomes a hassle and an emotional chore many of us simply choose to avoid. I had my fair share of experiences in that realm. When I shared with my manager my concerns that the COO of the company continually referenced my education in a demeaning way, and excluded me from his team meetings, she told me I was being too sensitive. This same manager also excluded me

---

3 *https://leanin.org/research/state-of-black-women-in-corporate-america*

from meetings and made sure I was the last one to find out about important updates within the company. I faced these issues often, insidious comments that I should smile more, or suggestions that by speaking out, I was 'angry.'

It was around this same time that a dream from my past began creeping back to me, slowly encroaching on my every waking thought. When I was younger, I'd been deeply intrigued by the idea of becoming a therapist. At 31, I'd completed my bachelor's degree in psychology, hoping that eventually, I'd be able to return and get a master's degree and work as a therapist. But I'd abandoned that dream for more realistic endeavors, and a career in HR. It was the safer choice, I told myself.

Now, it was all I could think about. I oscillated for a little while, unsure if it was the right decision for me. I wasn't sure if I wanted to become a student again at 54. But my yearning to help people heal became overwhelming, a calling that wouldn't be ignored. Regardless of my age, I had so much to offer. And besides, hadn't I already proved to myself that I wasn't too old to begin again? My entire life was a testament to that; I was *the* living, breathing example.

After doing some research, I found a program that seemed to fit my needs. I applied, and in 2019, I was accepted. I began the Master of Education in Counseling program, which was conveniently online, while continuing to work full-time. I knew it would be a lot of work, but I was committed to it. I knew that eventually, I'd back away from my corporate job to work as a therapist, but I was determined to accomplish as much as I possibly could while I was still there.

It took me a little while to adjust to the learning curve of online education, and the vast network of platforms I had to use. There was one to watch and attend seminars, another to submit video recordings and yet another to turn in assignments. I had classes twice a week, and weekly papers were due every Sunday by 11:59 pm.

I adapted to my new schedule, to the balancing act of work, school, and life. If I wanted to go out on a date or with my girlfriends on the weekend, I knew I had to get my schoolwork done early. I also learned to say no, to turn down plans I desperately wanted to say yes to. I was accustomed to sacrifice, having done it for others my entire life. But now, I was doing it for me, for the sake of my well-being and to ensure I was putting my best foot forward in school and work.

Life was chaotic, but it was good. I was happy, managing as best as I could with my busy schedule. In 2020, life took an unexpected turn. When the COVID-19 pandemic struck, we were all collectively thrust into the unknown, into a world of fear and masking, of sanitizing groceries and shifting our jobs to the online arena. I didn't mind working from home at all. I found the office to be a bit of a hostile environment. I loved my work, but dealing with some of my co-workers and other workplace politics was something I was happy to avoid.

Then, on May 25, 2020, all of our worlds took another collective shift after George Floyd was murdered by a White cop. The Minneapolis police officer, Derek Chauvin, pressed his knee into George's neck for an alarming 9 minutes and 29 seconds, all while the 46-year-old father pleaded that he couldn't breathe. The country, and the world, rightfully erupted in rage. We'd watched similar encounters between Black folks and police for decades, to no avail. Nothing was changing in our nation.

I remember talking to my son on the phone after it happened. I told him how much I missed him, now that he was living outside of the U.S. But at the same time, that reality helped me sleep much more soundly at night. It was never lost on me that my son could have easily been any of the hundreds of Black boys and men shot by trigger-happy racists. DK had been living with me in Orlando in 2012 when 17-year-old Trayvon Martin was shot and killed by George Zimmerman just one town over. When I saw photos of Trayvon, with his hoodie and his wide, curious eyes, I saw DK. All of the Black parents I spoke with reiterated my fears: that could have been my son. George could have been our brothers, our fathers, our husbands.

Meanwhile, Zii was out on the frontlines in New York, attending all of the protests, handing out gas masks and fighting for justice. I was both proud of their courage and terrified that something might happen to them.

George's death dominated our conversations. With my family, my friends, and even my co-workers, it was all we could think about. I'd spend my work days chatting with a handful of other Black and Latino coworkers, whispering about how sick we felt, how disappointed we were that our company hadn't said a word about what had happened and the very real, very urgent pain we were experiencing. Soon after, the CEO began hosting listening circles to allow employees to express their feelings and share their experiences.

Not long after that, the same superiors who'd rejected my proposal to start a DE&I initiative a year prior jumped on the opportunity to benefit from the hurt of the Black community. I was conflicted yet I felt that it was my chance and my duty to spearhead an initiative that could lay the groundwork for sustainable change within the company. High hopes, I know. Despite all the new, additional work I was doing, my pay remained the same. A double entendre, as loud as any could be.

In hindsight, I should have run fast and far. I should have said, "Absolutely not," and reproached them for even asking me, one of the only Black people in the office, to take on the emotional labor of addressing racial inequities that *I* suffered from and that *they* were responsible for. I was part of the group that needed support, yet they were recruiting me to do the work for them. Still, I was truly passionate about DE&I, and I wanted to be impactful. I wanted my job to be meaningful and I wanted to be at the helm of real, consequential change, so I approached the new role with enthusiasm and vigor. I leaned into it, hard.

One of the first things they had me do was create some very generic programs and training cycles. I wanted to create more long-term, strategic plans of action. I was thinking about how we could embed the ideals of DE&I into our learning and development, and how we could see them represented in compensation and in our recruitment efforts. But they were less interested in these ideas. They needed performative projects that showed the public how much we cared about equity, without actually committing to any of those promises.

At around the same time the company was trying to go public, they upped their efforts. They began hosting town halls, where they had me speak about our goals and what the organization was doing. The feeling that I was a figurehead, an instrument they were using to portray the appearance of diversity without actually committing to it, increased steadily. When they went public on Wall Street, they asked me to be in attendance on their virtual stage, to essentially sit there quietly and clap. I was the Black face to give the appearance of diversity. Soon after, stock photos of Black and Brown people began to appear on the website, and I was tapped to write a variety of articles on DE&I.

I felt physically and mentally sick, thinking of all of the ways they were exploiting my image and ideas. I was actually deeply committed to the ideals of DE&I, I desperately wanted to 'move the needle forward', as they say. I wanted to create a better, more equitable company for other people of color, and for other Black people especially. I felt they were making a mockery of our struggle, but I was helpless to stop it. Not only that, I was working around the clock, trying to push for real change. I was exhausted, in every single sense: my body, my mind, my heart. If I wasn't at work, I would think about it. It became so all-encompassing, that I barely slept.

One day, I was driving home from work on Highway 423 in Frisco, about 15 minutes away from my house. It was rush hour, and all of the folks who worked in the city were heading back to the suburbs in droves. It wasn't until traffic had slowed down that I realized just how tired I was, sleep descending on me like a dark, looming cloud.

With every second that passed, my eyelids felt heavier and heavier and I struggled to keep them open. Alarmed by my sudden exhaustion, I opened my window, hoping the cool air would whip me awake. As the traffic slowed to a near halt, I started to fall into and out of sleep, my eyes closing as though weighed down by boulders. Then, a car would whiz by or the music on the radio would change and I'd snap awake. At one point, I dozed off and my car continued to march forward, slamming into the car in front of me, and that car proceeded to hit the car in front of it.

I began to tremble uncontrollably, in disbelief about what had just happened. *I'd fallen asleep at the wheel of my car.* I wasn't physically harmed, thank God, but my car was totalled and I was mentally and emotionally shaken. Long after the police came and left the scene, and the two other cars had gone, I was still sitting there, in a state of shock, bawling my eyes out at what I had just survived and how horrible it could have gone.

At that moment, I should have taken a step back from everything. I should have recognized that my body was screaming for my attention, for me to evaluate the route I was going down. But I didn't. I knew something was off, but at the same time, I had gathered too much steam to slow down now. I had to keep going, to keep pushing forward.

I think that some part of my brain felt that I'd already wasted too much time and that I couldn't afford to squander any more. It is of course never a waste of time focussing on your health; it's a necessity. But, sadly, I didn't recognize how dire my situation was at the time.

A little while after my accident, my company got a new Chief HR Officer. I had been working closely with the previous CHRO on my long-term DE&I initiative and had been preparing a presentation for the CEO. I spent countless hours working on the project, researching stats, and perfecting the language. When the new CHRO came in, I began to report to a woman from her team, someone she brought in from her previous work life who had no HR or DE&I experience. That woman proceeded to present the work I'd done to the CEO, without me. She excluded me from the meeting, unveiling my initiative as though it were her own. I was absolutely furious. I'd poured months of work into the presentation, only to have someone who hardly knew a thing about DE&I impinge on all of my painstaking and tireless efforts.

I was so upset, I began to feel like my chest was caving in on itself. Every time I tried to take a breath, it felt caught in my throat. I was so dizzy I couldn't even stand. I knew something was very wrong with me.

At this time, Zii and their new dog Nangi had come home from Brooklyn during the pandemic to live with me. So one day, I asked them if they'd go with me to the doctor's office for a checkup. I had never asked either of my children to accompany me to an appointment before, but for some reason, I felt terrified of going alone. Graciously, they agreed. When we got to the doctor's office, which was on the eighth floor of the hospital, I sat on the examining table, fidgeting nervously. Dr. Brown, a Black physician, entered the room and I felt an instant sense of relief. I'd always hated hospitals and clinics, but being attended by a Black doctor eased my nerves slightly.

Dr. Brown took my blood pressure and looked at me with concern. "Your blood pressure is sky-high, Cathey," she said, a hint of alarm in her voice. She said she'd wait a few minutes, that maybe it was just white coat syndrome causing me to be extra on edge, and then she'd take it again, just to be sure. But the second time, it was still pushing 200. She took off the instrument and said we should just talk. She asked me a few questions about myself, what I did for a living, and other questions like that. Then she tested it again. When the numbers hadn't decreased, she told me she was sending me downstairs for more urgent testing. She put me in a wheelchair and had the nurse roll me down to the ER.

I looked at Zii, and we were both clearly terrified. I tried to reassure them that everything was going to be okay, surely I'd be fine. But I wasn't fine. I was in a hypertension crisis, and the doctors were fearful I was on the verge of having a stroke or heart attack. They ran various tests to ensure I wasn't at immediate risk of either, before hooking me up to medicine to lower my blood pressure.

After being in the ER for a few hours, Dr. Brown returned and told me she wanted to admit me for the night, to ensure that I stabilized before going home. I told Zii that they should go home, to feed the dogs and get themselves a bite to eat too. They didn't want to go, but I insisted. We had two dogs at home who needed to be taken out, and truthfully, I needed a moment alone to process what I'd just heard. Little did I know, Zii needed that space too. As they would later tell me, as soon as they stepped outside, they burst into tears, terrified that they might lose me.

After Zii left, Dr. Brown continued to explain to me the seriousness of what I was experiencing, of my sky-rocketing blood pressure. And the reality of the past year came crashing into me.

After my divorce, I'd thrown myself fully and completely into my job. I'd always thought it was just my ambition, my desire to make something of myself that was driving me forward. But I began to suspect that perhaps I'd simply supplanted one kind of achievement for another. I'd sacrificed myself at the altar of my career instead of my marriage. From my hospital bed that night, I began to see the reality I'd been missing all along. I was replaying the cycle of my failed marriage, just with different characters. I was pouring myself wholly into my work, praying that my superiors would see my passion, recognize my talent, and make me feel worthy of their acceptance and love.

And now here I was, standing at the doorstep of death. I knew that if I didn't make a big change, and fast, I'd be dead before I knew it.

CHAPTER 7
More Life to Live

When we're young, we tend to treat happiness like something we need to earn, something that will magically appear at our doorstep after we've checked all of the goals off of our list of things to do. When I graduate from school, *then* I'll be happy. When I get that dream job, *then* I'll be happy. When I meet my soulmate, *then* I'll be happy. Our happiness in life is always conditional on an imagined goalpost that seems to move farther away the closer we inch toward it. And we often end up neglecting so much of ourselves in this futile pursuit. We become burnt out, exhausted, depleted and even ill trying to satisfy all of the conditions our happiness depends on. By the time we get there, we're far too tired to even enjoy what we've accomplished.

In 2021, this was the reality I was facing in my own life. My career, though at first fulfilling, had transformed into an environment that took from me more than it gave. I poured myself into it, believing perhaps naively that it would all be worth it in the end, that I'd be able to affect real change. I was accustomed to the act of sacrifice; it came naturally to me. And wasn't it worth it, to put my own needs aside for the possibility of creating a better world? This sacrifice was different, I told myself. I wasn't doing it in service of a man like I had for years with my ex-husband. I was doing it as an act of love for my people. Is there a greater cause than that?

But soon enough, the reality began to set in that I was nothing more than a puppet my company used to create the illusion of diversity. And that's when I began to feel sick. By the time I ended up hospitalized with sky-high blood pressure, I'd stopped believing in the fantasy of changing corporate America. As I sat on a hospital bed, thinking about how dire my situation was, my doctor entered the room, ready to chat. She'd run tests to make sure I wasn't at immediate risk of having a heart attack or a stroke. I was in the clear for the very near future, but she placed me on hypertension medication for the first time in my life. She told me that she wanted to discuss the cause of my stress to determine what was going on with my health.

As I described my work environment, my doctor nodded, taking notes. I told her about the hostility from some of my co-workers, the tokenization and exploitation of my identity by my superiors, and the days and nights spent developing diversity programs only to have them passed off as someone else's work. I could feel myself getting worked up. My doctor diagnosed me with high stress and anxiety, resulting from my work. She wrote me out a note to take a leave of absence from work for health reasons and recommended I take a few months to myself.

At first, I was extremely resistant to the idea. Since my divorce, my life had mostly revolved around my work. Plus, I'd never known any Black women, or Black folks in general, to ever take a sabbatical. It didn't seem like something 'we' did. We didn't slow down or take breaks. We didn't rest. We swallowed whatever the world threw at us and kept moving.

Eventually, after some convincing from my doctor, I relented. I was *tired*. Plus, I was still in school, so this would at least give me more time to focus on my program. For the first few days of my leave of absence, I didn't know what to do with myself. I walked around my house, tidying things up or sitting on the couch flipping through the TV channels. But I got bored of that quickly and began searching for other ways to fill my time. Since I was little, I'd always loved gardening and many of my family members had green thumbs. As a kid, I'd spent many long, painstaking hours watching my dad care for our yard, carefully tending to his flowers which started at the driveway and continued all the way to the carport. And since I'd bought my own house in Dallas, I'd gotten back into the habit of growing things too.

Now, I jumped back into the hobby with both feet. It was a labor of love and patience, and one that I felt mirrored my own life and progress. For many people, gardening is too slow, too arduous and exacting, and they lose interest quickly. I, on the other hand, find peace and comfort in the measured, deliberate pace. Blooming only happens when the seed is ready, when its environment is prepared to welcome its growth. The soil needs to be nourished, the seed cradled by warmth and nutrients. I feel honored to be part of this life-giving practice and to be one with the earth.

Before long, my garden was a lush, verdant field of green. I grew cucumbers, tomatoes, squash, peppers, okra and melons. I had several varieties of roses and other flowers. I shared the fruits of my labor with my friends, family and neighbors. I learned how to can produce, and I soon had a healthy collection of jarred peaches, peppers and okra, which I gifted to those I loved. As life flourished around me, quite literally from my hands, I began to feel better, my health returning to me in the slow but deliberate pace of my overflowing garden.

A new routine took over my life. I'd wake early each morning and spend some time with my hands in the soil, just grounding myself. Then I'd go for a short walk, before coming back inside the house to journal. I began thinking more holistically about what made me happy in life. I thought about the things that brought me peace and joy. What would it look like to live a life that sustains rather than consumes? I tried to think of when I had felt the most alive, the moments that had made me excited to keep living. How could I move towards more of that, to lengthen those moments into hours, and eventually, into my entire life?

I kept going back to a trip I had taken to Panama a few years earlier, after my divorce. I was awed by the country, by the stunning landscape and beaches, and by the overwhelming kindness and generosity of the people. While I was there, I'd momentarily entertained the idea of maybe relocating.

Panama was close enough to the U.S. that I could easily return whenever I needed to. They used U.S. currency so I wouldn't have to worry about exchanging money or converting numbers back and forth in my mind. The weather was warm and sunny all year round, which vibrated well with my intolerance of the cold.

Maybe one day, when I've saved enough money and gained enough life experiences, I can do it, I told myself. When I returned to the U.S., work and all of my other responsibilities rushed to the fore and the desire to live abroad was pushed to the back of my mind. But now, as I gave myself space to explore what I really wanted from life, it kept returning to me in waves.

First, it was just a whisper, a murmur in my mind asking 'W*hat if?*' But eventually, it grew louder and louder, transforming into 'W*hy not?*' Work wasn't an issue. My children were grown up and out of the house. My master's program was online, so that wasn't a problem. Other than my home, I had nothing tethering me to Dallas or to the U.S. And even that could easily be remedied.

I thought about Elizabeth Gilbert's book *Eat, Pray, Love*. I loved the idea of taking a trip like that, of traveling to discover myself, to finally live life fully. But like taking a sabbatical, I didn't know anyone who did things like that. Rest felt superfluous, like something I hadn't quite earned (as if it is something you need to work for and not something you have always deserved). But the more I thought about it, the more the idea grew on me. I rejected the resistance that crept into my mind, the voice that told me, 'We don't do this.' Says who?! My people deserve rest. We deserve light, easy, fun lives where we travel and we eat and we pray and we laugh. We deserve joy. We deserve all of the things that we've been told for so long are out of our reach. I thought back to the whole of my life, the things I'd sacrificed because I believed so strongly in the idea that *this is what we're supposed to do*. That hadn't brought me happiness. I found happiness when I pursued it. And now, I wanted this. I wanted to move to Panama.

I began making small inquiries, researching the housing market in Dallas, looking up flight prices, and scrolling through apartment listings in Panama City. And the more I learned, the more confident and excited I felt about the possibilities.

I was 56 years old and in the prime of my life. Why would I wait till I was decades older to pursue a dream I was perfectly capable of acting on now? I had the physical capacity. I had the resources. I had curiosity and passion for life. There was no reason not to move forward with this dream.

I was working out in the garden one sunny afternoon, weighing the pros and cons of moving as I dug out handfuls of dirt. I stopped suddenly, wiping the sweat from my brow with the back of my hand. "I'm moving to Panama," I said out loud, the realization settling over me like a warm blanket. It felt less like a decision I'd made and more like a fact I'd simply accepted. This was the next step in my journey, the destination God had been leading me to for years.

When I finally hired a real estate agent to help me sell my house, I did feel the smallest pull of hesitation. That home had represented so much for me. It was the first one I'd ever bought before, all on my own. I'd lived there for 5 years, and it had been my comfort and my solitude, the space where I blossomed into the confident and courageous Cathey that was now moving to Central America. I really loved that house. Still, I knew that if I decided to move back to the U.S., I could buy another house and as long as I was in it, I'd be able to build just as many good memories there too.

At the time, Zii and their dog Nangi had moved in with me temporarily. They helped me pack up the entire house, which turned out to be more challenging than I'd anticipated. You never realize you have hoarding tendencies until it's time to throw away something you've owned but haven't used for years (or until you see the full gamut of holiday decorations you've accumulated).

As I sifted through my things, thinking back to the memories associated with each one, I sorted them into piles: to keep, to sell, to give away. There were records I'd had for decades, even though I no longer had a device to play them on. I had art I'd collected over the years. Photo albums filled with snapshots of my children growing up. It was like taking a stroll through the recesses of my past. It reminded me of how much I'd been through and how far I'd come. It was strange because, in a way, I felt like I was just beginning my life. I still had so much I wanted to do, so much to accomplish. And yet, I'd lived an entire lifetime already. As much as I wanted to hold on to everything, I knew that letting go would both free me from the baggage of my past and help propel me into the future.

Zii took the lead in organizing a yard sale and selling my furniture. After giving my family and friends first dibs, the more valuable and expensive pieces were listed on Facebook Marketplace. Everything else was packed away into boxes and put in storage. On my final day in Dallas, I walked through the empty house, my hands grazing the bare walls. It looked so different without all of my things. It dawned on me that perhaps what I loved so much about this house was the love that I had filled it with. From the decor to the furniture, the scents and the paint colors, the house was all me. It had been an empty canvas, and I was the artist.

Now, a new family would get a chance to do the same thing, to fill the space with their memories, their sounds, and the smells and textures of their lives. As for me, I was off to create my next masterpiece, which as it turned out, was my very own life.

On the flight to Panama City, I tried to imagine what my new life would look like. I didn't speak Spanish, so that was already one challenge I was going to have to address, though I had my Google Translate prepped and ready. I also didn't know anyone there, and meeting new people was high on my list. Over the years, having a community was what kept me from floating down a dangerous path of self-destruction; my community was my anchor.

Despite all of my fears, I was overwhelmingly excited. If there was anything my past had taught me, it was that I could trust in my power. Even if everything else fell apart, I had myself to fall back on, and no one in the world had my back like I did… except for God. That combination of faith in God and trust in myself had carried me through some of the most difficult moments of my life.

One of the most poignant and crucial realizations I made in this season of my life is how transformational prayer has been to my whole world. I don't even mean prayer in the traditional sense, hands clasped, sitting in the pews of a church.

When I was in my moment of need, desperate for guidance, I took one step towards God. I asked Him to help me through the darkness, to lead me to the light. Since then, I've seen God in everything. I'm hyper-attuned to hearing His voice, to receiving His message. I hear Him in my favorite songs, in the sounds of my children's laughter. I see Him in the kind smile of a stranger on those days when I need a kind smile, in the way the trees breathe in unison with my breath. And prayers come to me as naturally and as often as an exhale. When I take a walk on the beach, the salty water lapping at my feet, or when I stroll through the aisles of the grocery store, I'm always praying. I'm always thanking God. A whisper of gratitude is permanently etched on the tip of my tongue. And my move to Panama only deepened my appreciation for life, for the gifts God had imparted to me.

There, I built a life I'd dreamt about since I was a little girl. I was able to find a gorgeous apartment in an excellent neighborhood. My building had a gym and a pool, and from my balcony I could watch the sunset every evening, the colors of the sky mixing and blending in a kaleidoscope of dappled sunlight. There were beautiful walking trails just outside of my front door and there were beaches, both on the Caribbean and Pacific, just short drives away.

In Panama, I was able to afford a life that was way out of my reach back in the U.S. I was able to hire someone to clean my apartment a few times a week, and even invested in a personal chef. If I needed a massage, there was a woman who would come to my house to relieve my sore and achy muscles, right in my living room. And it wasn't only the affordability of life there that made it so enjoyable. The people are so genuinely kind and generous.

The Panamanian people are very proud, and they carry a deep sense of love for their country. Afro-Panamanians in particular love introducing Black American expats to their country, customs, and celebrations.

There's a spirit of community and communal responsibility that I didn't feel as strongly in the U.S. (it existed in the communities I built with my peers, but not in a broader, societal sense). People took care of each other. It was enriching to witness and empowering to experience.

That said, I created my own little community there too. Panama has a large and thriving Black expat population, folks who moved there from the U.S. to escape the threat of violence and toxicity, or who were, like me, attracted to the simplicity and accessibility of a good life. I met a couple, Terri and Clarence, who were also originally from Alabama. We forged a strong connection and they quickly became like family to me.

Panama healed things inside of me that I didn't even know needed healing. For the first time in my life, I was able to focus completely on living. I wasn't preoccupied with achievement, with fulfilling some invented sense of success that drained my energy sources without ever filling them back up. I no longer sacrificed what I wanted for the happiness and satisfaction of others. I wasn't chasing false happiness or someone else's definition of a good life. I just lived, doing whatever my heart wanted, whatever most closely aligned with my soul's calling.

I strengthened my relationship with my kids too. DK and Zii had chased their dreams with so much ferocity and courage, and I felt proud that they were also able to witness me doing the same, after so many years of complacency. In so many ways, I learned to be brave by witnessing them, how they questioned and interrogated the things they were taught to want, and went after what they desired instead.

By now, enough time had passed after my divorce that we could speak more candidly and honestly about the marriage, about how our lives were before. I welcomed their questions and their curiosity and I was committed to maintaining strong and honest relationships with my kids. It saddens me to say it, but after Jason and I divorced, he became deeply estranged from his children as well. It's as if when he stopped being my husband, he also ceased to be a father, a reality that sits like an open wound in both DK and Zii. Despite his shortcomings as a husband, he was always a good dad, so to see their relationship fade away into a few half-hearted texts during the holidays was heartbreaking.

I hate to see my kids cloaked in the pain of their loss, especially because it is voluntary. DK and Zii are being forced to grieve a living person. Whenever DK comes to visit me, he pulls out our photo albums and flips through them. I knew how deeply he missed what we'd once had: a family unit. I wish there was something I could do to make it better, but Jason is his own person and I can't force him to be present for his children. All I can do is pray that whatever struggles he's facing that are keeping him from being a father will eventually come to an end. I've learned over the years that it's not my job to take on other people's battles. Their struggles are their own – pray, release, and give it to God.

I am still their mother though. Whenever they come to visit, I cook their favorite meals. I keep up the traditions we had when they were little, hanging their childhood ornaments on the tree at Christmas, repeating familiar prayers on Thanksgiving. Now that they are both grown, our relationship has evolved into something more like a friendship. We confide in each other and even seek each other's input on important life decisions. I will always be their mama and they will always be my babies. But now, I try to do my mothering from a distance, to respect and support their choices, even when I don't necessarily understand them. They celebrated my move to Panama and my decision to go back to school to become a therapist.

After living in Panama for two beautiful, evolutionary years, in December of 2023, I packed up my life and prepared to move back to Texas. With the schooling part of my master's program coming to an end and graduation approaching, I will begin collecting the required clinical hours to become a licensed therapist.

I don't know what the future holds for me, but I feel excited to step into it, to begin this next chapter. Being a therapist has been a lifelong dream of mine, one I started when I was 18. I've lived so many lives between then and now. I'm 58, and 40 years have passed since I first embarked on this journey. I know how transformative therapy can be. I know the healing powers of this practice; I've experienced it firsthand. I've been down in the depths of hell and therapy was the ladder that helped me climb (and sometimes claw) my way back out. I know what it feels like to lose trust in everything and everyone, to view death as a gift and a salve. And I know what it's like to get to the other side of that seemingly insurmountable mountain of grief.

I have the privilege and honor of being able to look back at the whole of my life, to see with eyes wide open all that I've been through, all that I've succeeded in overcoming. There were so many times in the past that I wanted to give up, to simply dissolve into nothing. When I look back at my past lives, my heart breaks for all of the pain that girl and later woman endured. But all of my failures and hardships have brought me here, to this moment in my life.

The lesson isn't that suffering is necessary (though in a sense, and in a way, some of it is), but that it is temporary. It is a chapter in an otherwise long and manifold story; that is the very essence of life. There is pain punctuated by happiness and happiness punctuated by pain. There is sadness and grief that feels in the moment as if it will spiral down endlessly, forever, and there is joy that feels like ecstasy, that reminds you of all of the reasons why life is worth living.

No matter where you are in your journey, it is never too late to pick up the pieces of yourself and start again. Despite the societal pressures to believe that you're too old to begin anew, or to press the reset button, it's just not true. I say this as a woman who has done just that several times now. Life doesn't stop moving forward when you reach some arbitrary age, it doesn't cease to offer you the opportunity to have everything you've ever wanted. Every ending is a beginning. We've all heard the saying that when one door closes, another one opens. The thing is, you have to close and open those doors yourself, girl! The life you want won't simply happen *to you*. It will happen *for you*.

As long as you continue to pursue life, you will find something to be pursued. You can have that dream job. You can fall in love again. You can travel the world, wear that dress, take that pottery class, buy that house. You can rest and chase joy with the same passion and fire that you chase ambition. But the very first thing you must do is choose yourself. Believe that your life is worth fighting for. Trust in the prospect of a more beautiful future. And then run towards it.

I've lived a fuller, happier life in my 50s than I did in my 20s and 30s combined. I am now nearing 60, and yet I firmly stand in the belief that my life is just beginning. I still have so much to offer, and I know that the world has so much more to give to me. If there's anything I've learned in this long, storied life of mine, it's that sometimes you just have to open your hands and your heart to the possibility of change, of improvement. I wake up every morning and decide who I want to be and what I want from my life. I don't know what the future holds for me, or who or what I'll be in one year, let alone one month from now. But I do know that as long as I have another breath to take, there is more life for me to live.

Printed in the USA
CPSIA information can be obtained
at www.ICGtesting.com
LVHW090232091024
793326LV00002B/199